D0502723

SURFACING

SURFACING

FROM THE DEPTHS OF SELF-DOUBT TO WINNING BIG & LIVING FEARLESSLY

SIRI LINDLEY

WITH JULIA BEESON POLLORENO

Boulder, Colorado

For M, always my rock and biggest supporter

velopress®

3002 Sterling Circle, Suite 100
Boulder, Colorado 80301-2338 USA

Distributed in the United States and Canada by Ingram Publisher Services

A Cataloging-in-Publication record for this book is available from the Library of Congress.
ISBN 978-1-937715-52-6

For information on purchasing VeloPress books, please e-mail velopress@competitorgroup.com or visit www.velopress.com.

This paper meets the requirements of ANSI/NISO Z39.48-1992 (Permanence of Paper).

Art direction by Vicki Hopewell
Cover design by Pete Garceau
Cover photographs: Erik Isakson, front cover and cover flap; Timothy Carlson, back cover
Photo section: Courtesy of Siri Lindley, pp. 1–3, p. 6 (top), p. 8 (bottom), p. 13 (top) p. 16 (bottom); Rich Cruse, p. 4; Timothy Carlson, p. 5, p. 6 (bottom), p. 7, p. 8 (top), pp. 9–11, p. 13 (middle, right), pp. 14–15, p. 16 (top); AP Photo/Keystone, Fabrice Coffrini, p. 12

16 17 18 / 10 9 8 7 6 5 4 3 2 1

I saw the angel in the marble and carved until I set him free.

—MICHELANGELO

CONTENTS

1

UPENDING

THE DAY I WAS BORN—May 26, 1969—my dad, Peter Lindley, came to the hospital with arms loaded full with clothes and toys fit for a little boy. He'd done the same thing when my sister, Lisa, was born two and half years earlier, and both times was crestfallen to learn that my mom had given birth to a baby girl. They named me after my great-aunt, the sister of my Norwegian maternal grandfather, Erling Naess, a shipping baron who had been knighted. Siri, derived from the Nordic name Sigrid, means "beautiful victory."

My first night home from the hospital, I slept from 7 o'clock in the evening to 7 the next morning. My mom kept checking on me to make sure I was still breathing. A 12-hour sleeping jag is highly unusual for a newborn, but it became my standard. While my older sister had cried all night long, I never fussed, day or night—I was a preternaturally easygoing and happy baby. But once every few months, I would scream at the top of my lungs for no apparent reason. I'd get beet-red in the face and cry inconsolably for hours on end. After checking to make sure I wasn't being stuck with a diaper pin, my mom would call the doctor to come over to the house and look me over. Without a medical explanation for my outbursts, my mom concluded that I just needed to blow off some steam after being so well behaved all the time. Aside from those perennial episodes, I was totally content. As an infant, I'd spend hours suspended from the doorway in my Jolly Jumper. I'd bounce up and down, pushing off the ground with my tiny legs. Mom says it was the precursor to becoming a great athlete.

My mom, Astrid, was stunning. She had carved cheekbones and a wide smile, long blonde hair, blue-green-hazel eyes, and a lean, fit physique. Dad was classically handsome and a star athlete who had been captain of the baseball, football, and hockey teams at Yale. (He'd been drafted to play baseball in the Major League but opted to travel around the world instead.) They met on a double date in New York City, right after my mom had returned home after attending university in Switzerland. On the date, Mom was supposed to be with the other boy, but she hit it off with my dad, who made her laugh until it hurt. He was the life of any party, always engaging people with his quick wit. They shared a passion for sports and an upbringing in Greenwich, Connecticut, so the relationship felt immediately comfortable and compatible. They were married a year later, and my sister arrived before their first anniversary. My mom, whom I've simply called "M" for years, was just 20 when Lisa was born.

My best memories as a little kid took place in a cheery little yellow house on a quiet cul-de-sac on Plow Lane in Greenwich. Cozy at just 1,500 square feet, it had powder-blue shutters and a rustic wood fence encircling the front yard. I can still feel the warmth of the living room, where we spent most of our time as a family. It had a red couch and a matching recliner that Dad always sat in, blue shag carpet, a large brick fireplace, and honey-colored walls. Dad would bounce me on his knee while Cat Stevens music played from the large stereo. We spent hours playing Candyland and card games as a family, and Mom would dash between the living room and kitchen to bring us snacks like Dad's favorite, artichokes dipped in melted butter. She would set the platter in front of him, and he'd thank her and tell her how beautiful she looked. "Damn, Bird, you look good," he'd say in his New York accent. Despite being only a toddler, I remember feeling surrounded by love and lightness in that tiny house.

There was also a little pond and a huge weeping willow tree. We would spend hours playing beneath that tree on warm summer evenings. We'd splash around all day long in the kiddie pool and chase our two shih tzus and cat around the backyard. My dad had rigged up a trolley in the front yard that swung us between two tall pine trees. Before I was four years old, he had taught me how to swing a bat, throw a ball, and ride a bike with training wheels. He was endlessly patient and passionate about sharing his love of sports with his girls, and both Lisa and I were drawn to anything athletic.

One of my happiest enduring memories is our annual family visit to Playland in Rye. The amusement park was on Long Island Sound, and we'd ride the donkeys and the miniature train. Every birthday, from the time I was 4 to 10 years old, my mom took me to Playland. I could bring five of my friends, and she would carry a bag filled with extra pairs of undies, knowing that with all the excitement and the exhilaration of the rides, we would all pee our pants at least once.

Another favorite family spot was Old McDonald's petting farm, where we'd go on hayrides and visit all the animals. My lifelong love of animals started there.

Every summer we would visit Point O' Woods on Fire Island in New York, where my mother's family had a home. She'd been going there since before I was born, and it was the ultimate family summer vacation spot. There were no cars on the island, just bicycles and surreys. We'd be there with my mom and her family during the week, and Dad would join us on the weekends.

When Lisa was a year old, M decided to put her multilingual talents to work and got a job as a secretary to Bill Fugazy at Fugazy International Corporation, a successful travel agency in Manhattan. At the company's height, it booked in excess of $100 million in travel annually and had 35 agencies throughout the United States. Three days a week, she would meet Mr. Fugazy at the train station, climb into his chauffeured Lincoln Continental limousine, and take dictation as they made the drive into the city. She would spend the day doing a host of secretarial duties, including a lot of translation work (M is fluent in French, Italian, German, and Norwegian), and take the train home at the end of the day. Some days her assignment was to act as Big Apple tour guide to foreign clients.

My parents began hosting international au pairs so that there was someone to look after my sister and me on days when Mom worked in the city. The au pairs were allowed to stay in the United States for only one year on a visitor's visa. Our favorite was our first one, Hermine, a maternal and sweet German woman. Toola from Iceland was pretty and shy. Christina from Norway was clearly in America to find a man to take care of her. She met my mom's brother on her first night with us, and they had a date the next night and ran away together a week later. They got married and had two boys but were divorced after seven years.

Sometimes, under the watch of the au pairs, Lisa and I would get into some nasty fights. We were total opposites—she was rowdy and mischievous, while I was shy and docile—and when I became old enough to defend myself, we clashed ferociously. Once, after chasing me around with a hot curling iron, she locked me in my mom's closet and forgot about me, and the au pair was too busy making out with the boyfriend she'd invited over to notice. Even as a young child, I always saw Lisa as physically strong. That was probably why I didn't resist when she insisted on shaving me from head to toe in the bath one night. We had often been teased by other kids for being hairy (we both had Dad's dark features, abundance of body hair, and big, bushy eyebrows), so Lisa took matters into her own hands, with me as the guinea pig. She was confident, overpowering, and indestructible. Part of me really wanted to be that tough.

Even though Lisa was bigger and better at everything, I found myself swept up into the pageantry and drama of sports. For as long as I can remember, I've been transfixed by the Olympic Games. Lisa and I joined forces to compete against the Polansky sisters for medals, and we were intense competitors. I would put my heart and soul into winning events like the "paddle the raft across the pool," run relay,

H.O.R.S.E., tennis, soccer, and roller skating. I desperately wanted to be the champion and stand atop the Olympic podium.

While being a mom brought her a lot of satisfaction, M's job and the experiences it afforded brought a Technicolor punch to her monochromatic domestic life. Mom's boss, Mr. Fugazy, who was well on his way to transforming the family travel agency into a multifaceted transportation company, ran with the city's social elite—Bob Hope, Lee Iacocca, Mayor Ed Koch—and often brought M along to charity galas, celebrity golf and tennis tournaments, and other high-profile civic events. Any man would have been proud to have M on his arm, and she was an attentive listener who could strike up an easy conversation with anyone. She was the ideal companion for glittery high-society affairs.

While my dad was content working his 9-to-5 job as a Merrill Lynch stockbroker and reading the Sunday paper at the kitchen table, M dreamed of traveling the world and meeting interesting people. Still, they never fought or showed any signs of tension. My mom carried on steadily in her companionable but vapid marriage.

About a week before M's 33rd birthday, Mr. Fugazy invited her to a black-tie gala where Frank Gifford was serving as master of ceremonies. Gifford was one of the biggest celebrities of the day, a Pro Football Hall of Famer who had played for the New York Giants from 1952 to 1964 before turning to a second career in TV broadcasting. In a newspaper eulogy after his 2015 passing, he was described as "a gleaming hero of sports and television in an era when such things were possible, who moved seamlessly from stardom in the Giants' offense to celebrity in the broadcast booth of *Monday Night Foot-*

ball." He was a very big deal, and he had the charisma and looks of a Hollywood star.

The evening's program was already under way, and the hum of quiet table chatter filled the pauses as Frank spoke out into the elegant ballroom. As a waiter reached over M's shoulder to refill her wineglass, Mr. Fugazy turned to her.

"Astrid, your birthday is coming up!" he said. "Whaddya want me to get you as a gift?"

Without hesitation, my mom pointed to Frank on stage and said cutely, "I'd like that, please," like a child at an ice-cream counter.

Mr. Fugazy gave a sly smile and reached for his scotch.

Days later, he hosted an intimate dinner party in honor of the birthday girl at his Upper West Side penthouse apartment. Mom couldn't hide her surprise—and giddiness—when Frank Gifford walked through the door.

M said they didn't really like each other at first—she found him aloof, conceited, and arrogant, and he thought she was giggly, verging on ditzy. But about a month later, she went to the 1974 Super Bowl in Houston with Mr. Fugazy and reconnected with Frank, who was there for *Monday Night Football.* This time, there were fireworks. Frank was married to his first wife, Maxine, who was mostly homebound at the time due to multiple sclerosis.

Falling for Frank gave M all the incentive she needed to leave Dad. After seven years of marriage, and to his utter devastation, she filed for a divorce. I was four years old.

Frank was amazing to Mom in the beginning—he wooed her, showing her the good life that she'd previously only imagined. They went on extravagant vacations and stayed up late, talking about current events or nothing at all. She was happy to be on the arm of such a handsome, successful man, and he made her feel chosen, special.

But even as a young child, my feeling of foreboding that accompanied Frank's entrance into our lives was undeniable. The first time M introduced him to Lisa and me, I *felt* his presence more clearly than I saw him. He stepped into the room, and all color and light drained from the space. It was if I'd been basking in a warm, golden sunlight that was abruptly eclipsed by a dark, ominous cloud. I vividly remember an inexplicable sense of danger. I cowered behind my mom as she tried in vain to make an introduction.

Every time Frank came over, he'd try to talk to me, but I'd be completely unresponsive. Not only would I become mute and refuse to eat or drink anything in his presence, I'd pucker my lips into a fish face until one of us left the room. I didn't utter a word to him in the first two years he and M dated. My mom rationalized my behavior by saying that I was just ultra-shy and sensitive.

He still lived in Scarsdale, New York, with his wife and two kids, but he would come by the house randomly with his overnight bag and promises of marriage. This arrangement went on for about three and a half years.

One Friday, Frank told my mom he was coming for the weekend and that she'd need to send Lisa and me off to our dad's. We saw Dad every other weekend, and M really cherished her weekends with us. We'd already been looking forward to a full schedule of plans, and she hated the idea of disappointing us. Still, she sent us to stay with my dad at Frank's insistence.

Later the next day, Frank walked into the kitchen with his bag and told my mom he was sorry, but he had to go home early. She doesn't remember his excuse, but she was livid that she'd cleared her entire weekend only to have him bail out and head home to his wife. She told him that if he walked out the door, he shouldn't ever come back.

I didn't realize what had happened until a couple of nights later, when I awoke to the sound of her crying uncontrollably—sobs from the very deepest part of her. I ran and woke up Lisa, and we were both scared. We hovered over her, not sure what to do or say, and she told us to go back to bed. I was just a kid, but I understood that my intuition had become her devastating reality.

M booked a flight to Vail, Colorado, the same night Frank walked out. She decided we were moving. She had to get away from him, from the memories. She'd been to Vail before—her brother had a condo there—and it seemed as good a place as any to rebuild her life.

She flew to Vail and found a cozy little condo in foreclosure, and in a single day she managed to make an offer on the condo (which was accepted) and line up three part-time jobs: teaching French at the local middle school and aerobics to the employees of a ski resort and working as a saleswoman in a clothing shop. She flew home at 10 o'clock that same night, and two weeks later the three of us drove out to Vail. Dad was upset but didn't protest too much, believing that the move was most likely temporary.

Despite M's best efforts to position the move as a fresh start and create an inviting home for us, I was miserable. I didn't want to be separated from Dad, and it was the middle of my fourth grade school year. Valentine's Day came about a month after we moved, and while all my classmates were exchanging valentines, I sat there empty-handed. My only card was from the teacher—I didn't have a single friend.

As unhappy as I was in Vail, I was also relieved to get a new start with Frank out of the picture. M was still depressed a lot of the time, but I knew those wounds would heal. We were finally on the path to reclaiming the tight, harmonious family unit I'd been aching for.

Six weeks into our new life, Lisa and I were sitting at the kitchen counter, eating Norwegian meatballs for dinner, when there was a knock on the door. All of a sudden, Frank was standing in our doorway. He walked over and sat in the chair between my sister and me. Every bit as surprised as we were, M ducked into the bathroom to gather herself.

"I'm here because I love your mother and want to marry her," Frank said without any real greeting. "But I'm not going to marry her unless I get permission from both of you."

"Yeah! That sounds great!" Lisa chimed in without a moment's hesitation.

He turned to look at me.

"No! You can't marry my mom!" I blurted, making the audacity of his question crystal clear.

It didn't matter. Frank had brought his divorce papers along to show M, and six weeks later—four years into their relationship—he and M were married. The small wedding took place in Vail in the winter of 1978. Lisa and I walked down the aisle, each carrying a stuffed Snoopy dressed in a tux. I was shattered.

2

THE VOID

AFTER A TOTAL of six months in Vail, we moved back to Greenwich, Connecticut, this time into a modern-sleek behemoth of a house that Frank bought from a famous movie producer. It sat on the edge of an upscale golf course, and the driveway was the length of five football fields. It had all the Greenwich requisites—swimming pool, tennis court, pool, sauna, home movie theater, and three-car garage. Any kid would've been thrilled to live in a multimillion-dollar home like that, but I yearned for my cheery little yellow house on Plow Lane with its powder-blue trim and comforting memories. Lisa couldn't have been happier.

M nimbly stepped into the role of elegant wife to American Cultural Icon. She was an incredible cook, and it wasn't uncommon for Frank to call home at 4 o'clock in the afternoon and tell her to prepare her osso bucco or cannelloni because he'd just invited some politician, celebrity, or TV personality like Barbara Walters to dinner. She would frantically begin preparing for the impromptu dinner party, but it always turned out beautifully. I adored Barbara Walters—she would have me sit on her lap, and her warmth and interest in personally connecting with me made a lasting impression.

At Christmas, Frank and Mom would host fancy, fully catered dinner parties. There would be an "A" party and a "B" party. Frank always wanted to have M's friends (the B list) over first as a test run for the *real* event. (One of those lowly B-listers one year was Dan Burke, the husband of one of M's close friends and head of Capital Cities Communications, a major media company. The day after the party—at which Burke joked with other guests, "You know this is the B party, right?"—Capital Cities purchased ABC, so Burke became Frank's new boss.) Outside of these occasions, he'd say they didn't have time to socialize with her friends—she'd have to see them on her own.

Four years in a row, M and Frank were invited by famed real estate developer Bill Levitt, one of the richest men in America at the time, for a cruise aboard his 230-plus-foot yacht, *La Belle Simone* (made famous by a starring scene in the Anthony Quinn movie *Tycoon*). They'd tour the coast of Sardinia, Italy, or the South of France with Levitt, his wife, and usually one other couple, along with a crew of 36 to cater to their every need. Not one to lounge around lazily drinking and eating all day long, M would quickly grow bored. Sometimes she'd wake up before sunrise and swim to shore with her running shoes somehow in tow, go for a run, swim back to the boat, and return to bed before Frank woke up. She also loved going into the kitchen and hanging out with the chefs as they prepared fancy four-course meals. It's where she learned to make that killer osso bucco and homemade pasta that Frank always raved about.

Frank wanted M either on his arm or in his kitchen. She remained motivated to work outside the home, but he wouldn't have it. Always an enterprising go-getter, she began teaching aerobic dance classes for Jacki Sorensen's Aerobics Dance Company without him knowing. She choreographed and practiced workout routines in our basement while Frank was at work and taught at a nearby country club and high school gym. Her following grew into the hundreds, and some of her students made "Astrid's Mamas" T-shirts that they wore with pride.

For an entire year, Frank was in the dark. But then one night they were out to dinner, and Frank began to feel the stares of two women seated at a nearby table.

"Oh, come *on*, here we go again—I just want to eat in peace, and those two women keep looking over," he snapped.

Minutes later, as the pair shyly approached their table, Frank readied himself for the typical public fawning. Except they looked right past him and straight at M.

"Astrid!" one of the women started excitedly. "We are *such* big fans! We both love your class and have lost weight and feel so much better about ourselves, we just can't thank you enough!"

After a few minutes of animated chitchat, M thanked them, and they walked out of the restaurant. Frank's pinched expression showed his disapproval.

"Isn't my life *enough* for you?" he spit. "You have to go and do something on your own?"

Frank wouldn't tolerate sharing M with her daughters, either. He would get home from work around 5 o'clock, and we were expected to be out of sight for the rest of the night. If one of us dawdled downstairs, he would get on my mom about it, telling her he needed his space. Every evening, he'd drink his vodka on ice while he watched the evening news. I remember him whistling whenever he needed her—a short, crude pierce through the silent house—and she'd attend to him and then run upstairs and sit with us for a minute. Then she'd race back downstairs to be with him for 30 minutes, then come back up to us for a few minutes. It would go on like this all night.

I know those days were brutal for her. M later told me she felt like she was being pulled in opposite directions by two packs of horses. Frank had a lot of demands, and she didn't want to lose him.

Naturally, Frank insisted on her traveling with him for *Monday Night Football* games, and she would assume her place in a corner of the tiny broadcast booth. He fed off her validation and expected a lot of it. She chalked that up to him being a Leo.

In addition to all the work travel, there were a lot of vacations. M would tell me they were going away for a couple of weeks but that our housekeeper, Luzmilla, aka Lucy, would look after us. Many nights, Lucy wouldn't come home until after midnight—she was often tending to her ill husband—and once Lisa got her driver's license, she would drive to the train station and go into New York City and party all night.

Feeling completely alone on those excruciatingly long nights, I'd camp out in the kitchen, the only place I felt somewhat safe. It was the brightest room, and I drew comfort from visions of my mom baking cinnamon rolls and banana bread for breakfast or rolling out her homemade pasta dough. The terror I felt those nights was tempered only by the whisper of her presence in the kitchen. There was always a vase of fresh flowers on the large oval table, which was surrounded by white wicker chairs with a yellow floral pattern on the cushions. Mom kept two kitchen drawers stocked with Twinkies, cookies, chips, and Oreos for me. I would sit in a wicker chair with my knees tucked tight into my chest, my arms wrapped tightly around myself. Surrounded by our dogs—Charlie was a golden retriever, and we had two playful shih tzus, Fifi and Suzi—I'd stare into the small TV, wondering in earnest if anyone was ever going to come back. The driveway lights were activated by a motion sensor, and anytime they'd flash on, I'd come out of my skin.

When M was away, I would try to sleep in Lisa's room. I'd beg her to just let me touch her with one outstretched finger—I desperately needed to feel contact with another human being—and she'd slap it away. So I'd go into Lucy's room, where she'd be watching her Spanish soap operas. I'd flop onto the bed, which was always covered with stuff—sewing supplies, newspapers, clothing—and beg her to just let me lie there. I learned how to manage all the alone time, but I needed some kind of assurance that I wasn't totally isolated. A couple of times, Lucy let me drift off to sleep to the sound of her telenovelas.

Every now and then Frank would let M off the hook for travel, and on those nights I'd sleep with her. We'd have all the dogs with us, and in the morning we would read the comics in bed. Those sleepovers made up for everything—it felt like someone had tossed me a life buoy after weeks of floating at sea.

I often had trouble sleeping even with M at home. She'd make me a huge peanut-butter-and-Fluff sandwich, bring it up to me with a glass of milk, and stroke my head. We would talk about the day, which always helped mellow my anxiety to the point where I could sleep.

One night I remember feeling an intense swell of emotion, and I *had* to tell M that I loved her—I'd never said it before.

She'd just finished tucking me in and was starting for the door.

"Mom?" I whispered.

"Yeah?" she said.

I didn't say anything for a few seconds. All of a sudden, I felt scared and vulnerable.

'What is it, honey?" she pressed.

"I love you?" I stammered.

She walked back over to my bed and gathered me up in a tight hug. We both sat there crying for a minute or an hour—I can't remember.

My emotions, anxieties, and fears were hard to process, let alone communicate, and most of the time I kept things bottled up. My mom had no idea of the depths of my anguish—how alone, scared, and fragile I felt.

Frank the perennial celebrity spokesman was under contract with Standard Brands (now Nabisco), which had a liquor distribution arm, so each month a huge truck would pull up to the house, and the driver would unload a dozen cases of wine and liquor. And a ton of Planters peanuts.

Lisa was the biggest beneficiary of that sponsorship deal. When M and Frank were away, she would throw wild parties in the basement and force me to act as bartender. I was 12, and she was almost 15. (Dad once bought shots for Lisa in a restaurant bar in Colorado and told her she needed to learn what it felt like to get drunk, probably to discourage binge drinking, but his plan clearly backfired.) I'd be mixing random amounts of booze, trying to avoid eye contact with anyone, while Lisa's friends danced to Meat Loaf and got sick in the corner. An hour before Lucy was expected home, Lisa would drunkenly kick everyone out, and we'd clean up as best we could and hope we wouldn't get caught. If Lucy ever suspected anything, she never said a word to Frank or my mom (which would only have begged the question of where she'd been).

Unlike Lisa, I was embarrassed to have anyone over to our house. Even to this day, when people ask me where I grew up I say Rye, New York, because Greenwich connotes an affluent lifestyle that I have never identified with, never really wanted. Frank came into our lives, and everything became about money. He and my mom would come home from a trip with jewelry, trinkets, stuffed animals—all kinds of gifts—and I would thank them and push it all aside. Lisa loved it.

Frank had a hard time showing affection or consideration by any means other than his wallet. He flew us out to Vail on a private plane, and he bought me my first car, a green Volkswagen bug, when I turned 16. But he couldn't buy my affection or confidence in him. If anything, his money fueled my distaste for him and all he represented—a lifestyle that swept my mom out of town for long trips on luxury yachts. With Frank, the pendulum swung between absolute neglect of his stepdaughters and stifling interference.

One night we were eating dinner on the porch, and I was wearing a white Izod shirt, my wardrobe staple. Frank was sitting across the table.

"Look at those nice little titties you're growing, Siri," he said casually.

It took me a few seconds to register his words. A prickly heat bloomed across my face. Instinctively, I jumped up and darted into the house in tears. I felt humiliated and loathed the fact that I was subject to his insensitive commentary. For years he didn't even want us in view—yet he felt he had the right to speak to me like that. I was inconsolable.

Frank followed me into the house.

"It's nothing to be embarrassed about. I'm just saying that maybe it's time to start wearing different shirts—ones that won't show your growing breasts like that," he said coolly, as if I should accept his fatherly advice with appreciation.

M was quick on his heels, trying her best to snuff out a rapidly igniting fire that was as fierce as it was unexpected.

"It's OK, sweetheart, it's just that he's noticing that you're becoming a woman," she cooed. Her very existence as both my ally and his doting wife was a tightrope walk in gale-force winds.

Frank continued to dip in and out of a paternal mind-set. On the whole, he took a greater interest in interacting with me. Maybe it was because I, unlike Lisa, didn't seek his attention or approval. I hated him from day one, but over time, I decided to make an effort.

I would come downstairs while he was watching the news and ask him questions. But I never acted needy or like I sought his love. I think he sensed that about me, and it made him try harder. Or maybe he found it refreshing that I didn't give a shit that he was a sports hero and famous broadcaster. Whatever the reason, he was typically more gentle and generous to me. Still, we lived by his rules, which at times seemed not only unfair but cruel.

I had very few friends in middle school and high school, but my best friend was Kay Cowperthwaite. She would come on trips to Vail with us, and from the ages of about 10 to 14, we had a two-woman band, which we dubbed Albatross. She played the guitar, and I was taking drum lessons. We were going to be the next Go-Gos. My mom bought me a drum set and told me to make sure Frank never found out about it, so I stashed it in the radiator closet. Kay would come over to rehearse "Sweet Home Alabama" and Billy Joel songs. Sometimes we'd take breaks to play tackle football, and more than once I took Frank's Pro Football Hall of Fame helmet out of its case and used it.

One day I was on my drums—it felt so good to get all my aggression out—and Frank came home early and heard me. He charged downstairs, his face bright red. He reminded me that I wasn't allowed to have drums—they were very unfeminine—and said I had to sell them. The next day, he placed an ad in the paper and unloaded them for $100. I was devastated.

I had a motorbike, a little Honda 50. I saved up my money—I always had little enterprises like a lemonade or coffee stand—and my mom was all for it but knew Frank wouldn't allow it.

"Not in my house," he said when she did feel him out.

She still bought it, and, as with the drums, she said Frank couldn't know about it. I hid it in the gardener's shed, somewhere he never went. My mom would go on long runs, and I'd get on my motorbike and follow her. I went everywhere on it, pretending I was in an episode of *CHiPs*. And then the day came when Frank decided he wanted to mow the lawn—something he'd never done before—and there was my precious motorbike parked in the shed. He was livid and told me I had to get rid of it immediately.

"Why? I paid for it!" I protested.

"It's too dangerous—do you want me to take you down to the hospital so you can see what happens to people in motorcycle accidents?" he said.

I learned later that Frank's son had been involved in a car accident and had suffered some brain trauma as a result. He didn't relent, and I grudgingly sold the bike to my cousin.

There was also Floyd's disappearance. All of my shirts had little holes around the neck because Floyd, my cherished lop-eared rabbit, would nibble on me as I carried him around. He lived in a cage that we kept just outside the bedroom Mom and Frank shared, next to the Jacuzzi tub and sauna. Every night Frank would go to this small patio area to smoke a joint. I knew he was annoyed by the rabbit droppings that periodically turned up in the house, but he didn't seem particularly bothered by Floyd. But when I went out to retrieve him one morning and found the cage door wide open, I knew it was Frank's doing.

My resentment and anger became more pronounced. Again, he had robbed me of something that brought me a glimpse of joy during a pretty bleak time in my life. I started to act out.

One day in the middle of winter, my friend Amy came over to hang out. We walked to the edge of the frozen pond on the golf course. I assured Amy it was frozen solid and goaded her into walking out onto it.

"Are you *sure* it's really frozen?" she asked tentatively.

"Yeah, it's totally fine!" I lied.

"Really?" she pleaded.

She took three steps before the ice cracked beneath her and she was submerged. Adrenaline pumping, I reached down and helped drag her out of the freezing water. The air temperature wasn't much warmer.

"Siri, I need to go home, I'm freezing!" she said through chattering teeth.

"No! You can't go home! We'll get in so much trouble for playing around the pond. You have to stay here and dry out."

I had some matches in my pocket—I'd started stealing cigarettes from around the house and smoking—and I lit a piece of scrap paper "for heat." Amy begged and pleaded to go home, but I insisted she stay, dismissing her suffering however dire she made it sound. So what if she had to feel a little pain? I felt it all the time.

We had a lot of rain the following spring, and no one was allowed on the carefully manicured golf course. I took it as an invitation to steal a golf cart and burn doughnuts onto the green. When the head maintenance guy spotted me and started his golf cart in pursuit, I put the pedal to the metal and then ditched the golf cart before running into my house. When Frank got the call about what I had done, he acted angry on the phone but didn't really say anything to me.

I was determined to assert myself and was fully numb to the consequences that might follow. I remember tying a girl in my neighborhood to a tree as some sort of club initiation rite and then leaving her there, helplessly tethered for an hour because I forgot about her. I threw rocks at people walking to the bus stop. I egged cars. It was perfectly timed as your typical preteen rebellion, but I was angry as hell. My mom was the only one to be spared my ire. Sometimes I would sneak under the neighbor's fence and pick flowers to present to M in a beautiful bouquet.

If I was caught doing something bad and Mom found out, I'd say, "I would never do that!" And she'd believe me because until then, that kind of truant behavior was out of character. I masked my darker side, but I was that girl. I felt resentful, cheated, and I didn't know how to sit with that.

What I really craved was oversight and discipline—something Lucy provided later when she caught me stealing Frank's cigarettes or speaking impolitely—but M was gone a lot, and my dad was no better at providing those things over the years. He was madly in love with Mom and too consumed by his own pain from the divorce to be the father I needed. He'd come pick up me and Lisa every other weekend in his convertible, and we'd eat junk food and stay up late watching *The Love Boat*.

Right after the divorce, Dad moved into a dumpy one-room apartment down the road. We called it the Roach Motel because it was infested. That was why we didn't stay with him at first. It was disgusting. One of the few memories I have of his apartment is waking up one day feeling super-excited because I was going to make my dad his morning coffee. I ended up spilling boiling water down my leg and going to the ER for a skin graft.

Dad moved to Rye, New York, about 20 minutes from Greenwich, after his dad died. He settled into my grandparents' house—a large Victorian with ivy growing up the sides and a spooky dilapidated barn out back. To this day, whenever I have nightmares, that barn is usually involved. We would go there every other weekend. He'd wake us up with Dunkin' Donuts, and Lisa, Dad, and I would play baseball and football and cruise the flea market in nearby Port Chester. Lisa and I would go up in the attic with our little cousin Lola and rifle through trunks of my grandmother Lucille "Lucky" Lindley's old clothes and play dress-up, but at night I was convinced that every nightmarish creature from every horror movie ever made lived up there. Sometimes Dad would take us to the Manursing Island Club, a stately private country club on Long Island Sound where we were members. They emptied the pool for winter, and Dad would plop himself in the deep end and spread out his *New York Times* and read inside the warm enclosure. I would sit beside him and read the comics.

Grandma Lucky had a house in Kennebunkport, Maine, and we would visit her every August—as a family of four before the divorce and then without M. I adored my grandma Lucky. She was always warm and loving to both Lisa and me. She loved sitting on her enclosed porch, which hung out over the Kennebunkport River, telling us stories about anything and everything. She knew how to hold our interest. She always had an ample supply of homegrown apples, peaches, pears, and grapes and tried to get us to eat it by the basketful, even if it was overripe with mold. My sister and I would look desperately at one another, not wanting to put the rotting fruit into our mouths but also unwilling to disappoint her. We would take it from her graciously and then throw it into the river when she wasn't looking. She loved dogs, and when her husband passed away from leukemia in his 60s, she tried to fill the void with her pugs.

The Bush family also had a home in Kennebunkport, and Marvin Bush (brother of George W.) became one of my favorite people. Everybody, of course, saw the Bushes as American royalty, and there was a ton of security surrounding their compound, but Marvin seemed like a regular guy who was always warm, considerate, and down-to-earth when we crossed paths. I usually felt invisible around adults, but he asked questions about my life and was always happy to indulge my inquisitiveness. He'd invite my sister and me to go out on the family speedboat, *Fidelity*, and I would sit at the tip of the bow and hang on for dear life as we flew through the waves. It was exhilarating, and I always felt safe because I considered Marvin a valiant and kindhearted knight who would take us on this incredible adventure and deliver us home, safe and sound. I remember writing letters to him when he went off to college, and later he and his beautiful wife, Margaret, seemed genuinely happy to see me each summer. He was the kind of person I wanted to be—respected, worldly, and successful but approachable, sincere, and compassionate. He made me feel like I mattered, and I knew I wanted to have the same kind of impact someday.

Several years after the divorce, my dad remarried after a brief courtship. His new wife practiced witchcraft and would host séances and routinely use a Ouija board. She also drank to the point of excess, which equally unnerved me. Her son, Johnny, despite being five years younger than I was, terrorized me—he kept Chinese throwing stars under his pillow, and if I ever made him mad, he'd threaten to put a spell on me or kill me with his Chinese stars. After convincing me that the house was filled with ill-intentioned spirits, he locked me in the attic. Thankfully, after four years Dad divorced Johnny's mom, and I was free of his cruelty.

Athletics were my lifeline amid the chaos of my family life. Having an outlet to channel my surplus of anxious energy was vital. In junior high, I played on the boys' baseball team, but more often than not I sat the bench or was stuck in the outfield, where I didn't see much action. My dream of being a professional baseball player gave way to a host of other high school sports—field hockey, ice hockey, and softball, initially. Competition allowed me to focus on something other than my fears and gave me a glimpse of my own resilience and work ethic. I learned I was more than just a tangle of nerves. While I was never the star of the team, I was a strong and versatile athlete, and, most importantly, I was beginning to appreciate what sports brought to my life—a sense of accomplishment and self-worth.

One afternoon early in my freshman year, the lacrosse coach approached me in the hallway at school. Coach Renee Spellman was an imposing figure. She had a big, barrel-chested frame supported by long, dark, muscular legs and wore a cardinal-red jacket with "Greenwich Lacrosse" embroidered over her heart. A whistle dangled around her neck, and she carried a clipboard under her broad biceps.

Coach Spellman had seen me running the 1-mile loop around our high school during field hockey practice. Because it felt good to run hard—the burn in my legs and lungs made me feel strong and alive—I was inclined to sprint the whole way. She asked if I'd ever considered playing lacrosse.

"Me? Lacrosse?" I stammered.

Lacrosse was Lisa's sport—she was the star player on the varsity team. Perhaps Coach Spellman thought that since Lisa was so talented, little sis might have some potential, too.

But she made it clear that it wasn't about Lisa.

"I've seen you during practice, and I think you're a tremendous athlete. I want you to play on my team," she insisted.

"My sister is the lacrosse player. I don't think I'd be any good at it," I demurred. I idolized Lisa—she was effortlessly brilliant in school and a natural MVP on the field—and I knew she definitely wouldn't want me cramping her style on the same team. Plus, I'd be starting softball in the spring.

But Coach Spellman wouldn't let it go. Every day she asked me to play on her team, casually dismissing my complete lack of knowledge or experience in the sport.

"I'll teach you everything you need to know," she'd say. "Just show up—I think you could be great."

After a week, I caved. I told her I'd give it a shot, fully expecting to humiliate myself and prove her dead wrong. But it turned out Coach was right—while I was no Lisa Lindley, I took to it quickly. I dove into lacrosse with energy, focus, and drive to be better. I spent countless hours after school and on weekends in the backyard with my lacrosse stick. And, as expected, Lisa was furious. Most practices she just ignored me. I relied on her to get home, and some days she'd warn me that if I wasn't outside the locker room in five minutes, she'd leave without me. I'd frantically rush to meet her, relieved that I'd taken just three and a half minutes, and she'd be gone. We lived 25 miles away from school, so I would have to wait alone in front of the high school for M to retrieve me as soon as she could, which sometimes wasn't for a couple of hours, depending on her work schedule.

But I wasn't about to give up my newfound passion.

Coach Spellman had a presence that made us stand up straight and hold our tongues. She was intense and intimidating and had a wicked sense of humor. To call us off the field, she'd bellow, "Bring it in, pig-dogs!" and if we ever goofed off, she'd punish us with an ungodly number of wind sprints. But I felt safe and steadied under her critical watch and sensed she was deeply invested not only in making me a team asset but also in steering me in the right direction. (I believe the platitude "tough love" was invented to describe Coach in two words.) I still don't fully understand what inspired her conviction and faith in my potential, but her insistence that I could achieve remarkable things in my life thrust me down a decisive path when I was standing disheartened and aimless at a critical crossroads. Coach was the first person to tell me that I needed to believe in myself, and she took every opportunity she could find to build up my confidence and develop my character. She asked if I was doing my homework and thinking about college. She kept me accountable and honest. She saw a sad, scared kid and cracked me open to let out a little light.

The only other person who had ever been so convinced of my athletic promise and shown that much blind faith in me was Uncle Boyce. Prior to marrying my mom's sister, he'd been a member of the

US rowing team that took home Olympic gold at the Tokyo Games in 1964. With his muscular shoulders, broad chest, and thick neck, he reminded me of the Incredible Hulk. He lived in Pennsylvania, but every July we would see him and his family on Fire Island, New York, where I'd sit on the sundeck of our rented beach house with Uncle Boyce and chat with him while he sipped a beer. One summer when I was 13, I had recently run a 5K in my polo shirt and baggy surf shorts and done pretty well, beating a lot of the grown women. Uncle Boyce took it as an opportunity to tell me I was a gifted athlete with a lot of potential. In him I saw someone who transcended the ordinary to leave an important legacy through sport. The promise in his words percolated in my young, searching mind on those warm summer nights.

Outside of sports, insecurity still inhabited every corner of my life.

My mom exuded confidence as she played the role of the good wife, but I've since come to know that she harbored insecurity of her own, though she was not allowed to show a trace of it when it came to her marriage.

"You have to accept the fact that women are going to be throwing themselves at me," Frank told her. "If you want me to fall out of love with you, just be jealous—it will turn me off completely."

So when TV personality Kathie Lee Epstein called M in 1985 to ask if it would be okay if Frank accompanied her to a charity luncheon, M conceded. Kathie Lee had met Frank when he'd guest cohosted on *Good Morning America* with her in 1983.

M thinks their affair started right after that luncheon date. Friends told her what was going on, and she was wise enough to see the signs for herself. Frank had numerous affairs while he was married to her, most with well-known people. A 2013 book by Johnny Carson's long-time lawyer, Henry Bushkin, claimed that Frank had an affair with Carson's wife (which she has categorically denied). When Frank was away, he'd call Mom at 9 p.m. and say he was going to bed, but in all likelihood he was heading out on the town. Considering the circumstances under which he'd met M, the infidelity was hardly surprising. The rules simply didn't apply to him. Who was anyone to tell him no?

With everything out in the open, Frank left again. The three of us stayed in the Greenwich house while M plotted our next steps. She was deeply hurt and humiliated, and the stories in the tabloid papers about the various women he was spotted with just turned the knife.

Eight months later, in 1986, Frank called M from Hawaii. He'd made a huge mistake, he said, and wanted her back. He insisted she get on the next flight to Oahu to join him there. Completely blindsided, Mom told him she and I were set to fly to Club Med the next morning for our own getaway. Canceling on me wasn't an option, she said. But Frank was persistent, and he told her I should come with her.

"Isn't saving our marriage a little more important than a Club Med vacation?" he pressed.

We stayed at a five-star hotel, where they put me in my own room and left me to play canasta with Frank's mom all day while they talked things through. I was 16 and never more disheartened and lonely.

During one of their beach walks, Frank told M that he had a great idea for how they could "put the spark back into the relationship."

"Let's get a divorce, and then I'll court you again!"

He said it with such conviction, like it was the most brilliant idea he'd ever had, and M went along with it.

A few months later, Mom was due to visit divorce court with Frank, thinking there was still promise for a rekindled relationship. A few days before her court date, she turned on the TV and saw Frank and Kathie Lee cohosting *Good Morning America* again. Her gut seized up—any fool could see they were crazy about each other. M immediately called her lawyer and asked him if she should request that the judge revisit the payout from the divorce. She hadn't asked for much, believing she and Frank would be getting back together and it was all part of his master plan.

But it was too risky to let a judge decide her fate. If the judge knew anything about football, he'd surely side with Frank. She decided to leave it alone.

Sure enough, when they entered the courtroom, the judge jumped out of his chair, brushing right past M in his beeline to Frank.

"Frank Gifford! I never missed a game—what an honor!" he said, vigorously shaking Frank's hand.

The day after the divorce was final, Frank and Kathie Lee got engaged. This time he was gone for good.

3

WATCHTOWER

MY MOM'S COPING MECHANISM in those early postdivorce days was exercise—a lot of it. First thing in the morning, she would power walk for an hour and then teach an aerobics class. After class she'd go on a bike ride and then swim laps at the pool before teaching another aerobics class. On Sundays I'd tag along for all of it. I was shackled by an acute paranoia that something or someone was going to cause her harm—she was too vulnerable to be without my constant oversight. She was in a lot of pain, and my worst fear was that I would lose her to it. That fear dictated my every thought and move, and I felt like it was my sole responsibility to keep her safe from the menacing depression. In my quest to make M feel secure and loved, our roles had reversed, and that self-imposed pressure on the flimsy psyche of a teenager, paired with all that physical activity, left me completely fried. We'd be out for a power walk at the end of a full day, and if M accidentally bumped into me or looked at me the wrong way,

I'd become incensed. I was at my wits' end from an exhaustion that permeated every cell of my body. Despite my recurrent unraveling and her struggle to heal from heartbreak, my mom still remembers this period fondly because we were making up for lost time. I could see that having me around lifted her spirits tremendously, which only added to the pressure I put on myself to protect her fragile mental state. While M never told me she needed me, there was no way I would abandon my watchtower post.

I rarely did anything outside the house—school and sports practice were my only outlets—and M and I grew deeply codependent. The only relief from my worry about her came when I was by her side, though I wasn't immune to the social pressures of high school. Once in a while I would go to a party. While my friends drank cheap beer and let loose, I sipped Gatorade, which I secretly poured into emptied beer cans. I wanted desperately to fit in and be liked, but the idea of losing control was out of the question. I had no desire to reenact those ugly scenes of kids getting wasted at Lisa's parties. I didn't need alcohol to make myself physically feel like shit—the worry would pile on top of me, wrenching my stomach to the point of nausea. The room would start spinning, and I'd have to call M to come get me.

I developed some obsessive-compulsive tendencies that stemmed from my constant worry. I would repeat a thought—a prayer, really—over and over again until I felt satisfied. *God, let us be okay, make us safe.* I'd recite my silent plea a dozen times or more. Or I'd flip the light switch on and off until it felt safe to stop. My strange behavior went unnoticed by my mom, but I was gripped by these compulsions that helped me create order of the chaos in my mind, if only for a moment. I began to feel like I was losing my mind.

Once a week, my best friend Kerry Bozza and I would visit the local retirement home, which was a welcome distraction. It let me get out of my head a little and focus on something other than how fucked up I felt. We would sit with the elderly people, and I loved seeing how excited and happy they were to have company. I grew especially attached to a sweet woman named Betty, and I was heartbroken when I showed up to visit her only to find that she had died.

While I attempted to orchestrate an insular existence for the two of us, M felt abandoned by all the people she used to call her closest friends—they'd all stuck by Frank after the divorce and were soon part of Kathie Lee's inner circle. Even Lucy had gone with Frank. During my junior year, we moved to Rye, New York, while Lisa went off to start her freshman year at the University of Colorado in Boulder. In the divorce settlement M got a modest house—that's it. The little home on Bird Lane was small but quaint, and it sat at the edge of Long Island Sound. My mom would walk the 200 meters to the water's edge to go night swimming. I had my own large bedroom and took over a smaller room to showcase the ribbons and awards that I had earned in sports. Down in the basement my mom built an aerobics dance floor, where she began creating her aerobic dance program that soon became a huge hit in the town and elsewhere. She was down there often, blasting Men at Work while choreographing fun and challenging workouts.

Frank may have assumed my mom would go straight to the tabloids with her side of the story, but she never considered airing their dirty laundry. The last thing she wanted to do was hash out all the painful and humiliating details in the press. Still, reporters kept badgering her. Once, when we went to Vail to get away, M was taking out the garbage when a reporter jumped out from behind the Dumpster and tried to get her to talk, offering a significant amount of money for an exclusive interview. She said no. Always no.

The move to Rye meant I was closer to Dad, and seeing him at all my games brought me a lot of comfort. A lifelong sports fanatic, he never missed a game, and seeing the pride on his face was deeply satisfying. His unshakable belief in me as an athlete took my motivation to new heights. Whereas my mom, an accomplished athlete in her own right, approached sports from the perspective of enjoyment, fitness, and emotional and physical release, Dad introduced a competitive ferocity. He would pace the sidelines and heckle loudly when he thought the ref made a bad call. A few times, he was kicked out. After each game, Dad would rehash every second in an animated hour-long play-by-play analysis. He *always* found something I could do better. I could've had the game of my life, and he would offer some piece of constructive criticism. His interest in my performance and athletic progression showed me he cared—and I did crave the attention—but it was also frustrating. I didn't want to hear about the things I'd done wrong; I was desperate to hear how I'd made him proud.

This continued throughout my four years at Brown University—Dad would drive three hours each way to be at every home game. My teammates grew to love my dad, too. He was part of a loudmouthed group of dads who formed a sideline cheering and commentary section. Mom made most of my games as well and balanced out my dad's zeal with her ever-nurturing nature. I had been more heavily recruited for ice hockey, but when I started my freshman year, the lacrosse/field hockey coach said I wouldn't be able to play ice hockey because it overlapped too much with the lacrosse season. I was devastated that I couldn't pursue both.

While athletics and a strong academic record weighed heavily in my Brown application, I'll never really know if Frank had any influence. Before the split, he'd insisted on taking me to visit Brown's campus and meet with university administrators. I remember feeling resentful that he had to impose himself on the process like some big shot—he wanted to take credit for anything positive that happened in my life. Again, he was marring something sacred that was supposed to be mine. Although I was also accepted at Princeton and Cornell (in those cases, the admissions staff didn't know I was Frank Gifford's stepdaughter), I've never been able to completely silence the nagging question of whether or not I earned that opportunity entirely on my own. But I also can't deny the fact that Frank's financial support made it possible for me to attend an Ivy League school. Dad had lost my college savings in the stock market, and there was no way my parents could have afforded it.

Leaving M for college was brutal. She assured me repeatedly that she would be fine and told me not to worry about her, but I still felt intense separation anxiety. I did my best to push the fearful thoughts out of my mind, and I called her from the dorm lounge every night. At the end of every call, she'd encourage me to go live my life and find the fulfillment and peace she felt I deserved. One thing I really loved about Brown was that I could choose to be evaluated using the conventional grading system (A–F) or a pass/fail scale. I opted for the latter and was energized by the autonomy and challenge to make the most of the open-ended opportunity. I was just as focused as the kids aspiring for straight A's. I arrived early to class and would sit attentively listening to lectures, soaking up the material like a bone-dry sponge. Everything was intriguing, especially my psychology-major curriculum. Why is the human brain wired so differently from person to person? Where do our fears and flaws originate, and how do they define us? Can we change our deeply ingrained thought patterns?

Studying psychology in college helped me get a handle on my obsessive-compulsive behavior. I learned about the mechanisms behind the condition and that I didn't have to live with it. I had to train my brain to make it stop. My self-prescribed treatment involved a lot of self-talk. *This shit has got to stop. It is not going to prevent your fears from happening—it will only feed them, further exhaust you, and make you look like a weirdo. Is that what you really want?* I wasn't healed overnight, but I could feel the vise beginning to loosen.

I thrived under the pressure of college life. I'd have weeks to complete a big assignment and would wait until the night before it was due to start working on it, and somehow it always came together. I felt enlivened by the summons to sink or swim.

Known around campus as a jock, I did my best to fit in. I dreaded the pressure to party all the time, so I was relieved whenever my lacrosse or field hockey team had to travel for a weekend game. When I did stay on campus, I would rally and go out with friends but never drank nearly the amount they did. There seemed to be no escaping the alcohol-associated angst. My sophomore year, I had a roommate who had a major drinking problem. I finally had to ask for help from Student Services when I woke up in the middle of the night to find her squatting in the bedroom closet, peeing all over her shoes.

By my junior year, I had begun to feel stability for the first time in my adult life. My classes and team sports were gratifying, and M had made incredible progress in her healing. She was busy running a successful dance aerobics company and teaching four classes a day. I could see her confidence returning, and that relieved a lot of the pressure on me. Ever the resourceful entrepreneur, she also created a series of audiotapes that guided people through an exercise walking program. Seeing her take control of her life during that difficult time gave me an awesome sense of pride and hope.

Dad was still coming to every home game, invariably a charismatic force of personality. I assumed the opposing team found him terribly obnoxious and was taken aback one day at a lacrosse tournament at William and Mary. Dad was pacing the sidelines, his usual antics on full display, when I heard a voice from over my shoulder.

"Who's *that?* He's hot."

I turned and saw the rival team's assistant lacrosse coach pointing to a guy across the field. My eyes settled on the figure she was pointing at, and I flinched at the recognition.

"Are you kidding me? *That's my dad,*" I said, aghast.

"Will you introduce me?" she replied coolly.

A former member of the US National Lacrosse team who was 28 years younger than my dad (and just four years older than I), she was at my side when he approached me after the game. He started right in with his usual analysis of my performance, and I cut him off brusquely with a rushed introduction before catching up to my friends. I started to jog, desperate to put as much distance between me and that painfully awkward interaction as I could—quickly.

At the end of the school year, I headed to Club Med for my summer job. I'd landed the seasonal gig after visiting Lisa the previous summer (my sophomore year) at the Club Med in Cancún, Mexico, where she worked as the land sports director, organizing various games and activities for guests. Someone looking after children in the Kids' Club had gotten sick, and the manager had asked my sister if I'd be able to fill in and stay an extra couple of weeks. I did, and they asked me to return the following summer, this time as the land sports director at their property on St. Lucia in the British West Indies.

Lisa and I had grown up going to Club Med with M every year, and I was always intrigued by these wildly dynamic extroverts who walked around the property, rallying guests to join in some scheduled activity or class. We'd be lounging sleepily in our bathing suits, and someone impersonating a cheerleader on a caffeine high would launch into an impromptu poolside pep rally. "*Who's up for a game of beach volleyball? Let's gooooo, guys! Time to earn that vacation meal!*" A textbook introvert, I'd look at them like they were aliens from a different planet.

And then it became my job to be that cheerleader. To say it was a stretch out of my comfort zone is a vast understatement—I was terrified. But because I was totally anonymous (and in suspended-reality mode), I allowed myself to be silly and young and carefree. Words can't describe how liberating it was. I'd never imagined I could make people laugh, entertain others, and inspire them to be active, and I realized that this fun, fearless girl lived somewhere inside me. For the first time, I didn't stress about what people thought about me. I fell for the chief of sports, a Mauritian guy named Singh. His great charisma and handlebar mustache more than compensated for his short stature. He made me feel good about the person I was at Club Med.

There was a Frenchwoman, Solange, who worked in the boutique on the property. She was stunningly beautiful—tall with short, funky hair and an exotic accent. She looked polished, confident, and classy. I would always say a brief hello when I passed her shop, and my heart rate would quicken for a moment. Every night, I would spend an hour getting ready for dinner, partly because I wanted to exude the same electric energy she did, but I also wanted to look my best to impress her. I didn't understand it, but she definitely stirred something inside me. When I found out that she had a girlfriend with her there at Club Med, my intrigue only grew.

One day during that summer stint at Club Med, I called to catch up with Dad. When a woman picked up, I thought I'd misdialed the number.

"Uh, hi, is my dad there?" I asked, poised to apologize.

"No, he's not here right now," she said in a matter-of-fact voice.

"Do you mind me asking who this is?" I asked, totally confused.

It was the lacrosse coach I'd grudgingly introduced to Dad.

My heart and head raced in tandem. She had moved in, and a year later they would marry. Part of me was relieved that he wasn't alone—I could see that she seemed to make him happy.

At the end of summer, I headed back to Brown, and while my camp-counselor persona stayed at Club Med, my confidence and self-esteem were nourished by those weeks away. My senior year, I told the field hockey/lacrosse coach that I missed ice hockey and was going to play on both teams since the ice hockey coach agreed to let me play varsity. The lacrosse coach threatened that if I tried to play hockey, she would do everything in her power to keep me on the bench. I knew I was an important player on our team, so I held my ground, telling her I'd do whatever it took to make her play me. Ultimately I was able to close out my senior year playing both sports. I was elected captain of the lacrosse team, which was a huge honor.

My friendship with Coach Renee Spellman continued well into my college years, and she came to a lot of my lacrosse games. I fed off her relentless positivity and calming assurance that everything was going to work out okay for me. I went to her house to visit during one of my trips home and realized she shared her home with a woman, Susan. It became clear that Susan was her partner, so I felt comfortable confiding in Renee that I was having thoughts that I, too, might be gay. She could tell I was anxious about it, and she encouraged me to face my reality with backbone and self-acceptance. "You were put on this earth to be happy, and you don't have a choice in this, so try to find the strength and courage to be who you are," she said. "People love you for the person you are, not the person you like." Once again, she could see that I was overwhelmed, and she made a point of being there for me. Seeing a gay woman who was widely respected and deeply content opened my eyes to that same possibility for me.

After graduation from Brown in 1991, I tried out for the US national lacrosse team. I got cut in the final round and was so disappointed that I hung up my lacrosse stick. I applied for a job as assistant field hockey and lacrosse coach at Princeton. The job interview was complicated by the fact that I had been offered admission to Princeton as an incoming freshman, accepted the offer, and then decided to go to Brown. I'd had to withdraw my application, disappointing the same people who were now conducting my job interview. Still, I ended up getting the job. My on-campus housing was a single room at the very top of a Rapunzel-like tower. It had windows on every side, offering a panoramic experience of campus life—industrious students scurrying to class, athletes fine-tuning their skills on the sprawling sports fields, magnificent Gothic architecture, and park-like beauty. Aside from the inspiring view, it was a Spartan existence, offering no more than a mattress, small couch, TV, microwave, and toilet. To get there, I had to take an elevator from the gym, where I showered. Nights were eerily quiet.

The Princeton coaches held me to a high standard. Fresh out of college, I was intimidated and nervous. They had a winning program, and I didn't want to make any mistakes. Being a part of that program made me realize what it took to be the best and perform under pressure, but after a year, I decided to pursue another opportunity—still coaching field hockey and lacrosse—at Lehigh University in Allentown, Pennsylvania. The head coach gave me a lot of authority and responsibility, and right away I knew it was a much better fit.

One afternoon Coach Spellman called to tell me she had cancer. It had originated in her thigh and had begun to spread. I went to visit her a couple times, and she never let on how much pain she was in or how serious her diagnosis was. When she was admitted to the hospital, I went to see her. She was breathing through an oxygen mask and wearing the Lehigh University baseball cap I'd given her. When I sat down on the bed next to her, she took off her mask and started singing, "*Nooo, I ain't gonna go now, no, I ain't gonna go nowww. . . .*" And then she slid the mask back over her mouth and drew a deep breath. It must've taken every ounce of her energy.

She was gone the next day. She left me a box of things from her desk—inside, I found a bell in the shape of an apple and a sports clock I'd given her years earlier. I was gutted by the loss.

I had a group of good friends who lived in Worcester, Massachusetts, and every chance I got, I would drive the five hours each way to see them. After a year at Lehigh, I decided I wanted to live closer to them—they were gay and made me feel wholly accepted and free to be myself. I applied for a job at the Worcester YMCA as the member services director. It was my first job that offered a real salary and health insurance. When they told me I would be making $20,000 a year, I thought I'd won the lottery. In my new role, I wore many different hats, but my primary responsibility was to recruit new members and run the fitness center. I also did some personal training, taught water-aerobics classes to seniors, and led a gym class for the mentally challenged. It felt like a big extended family. I worked 60-hour weeks and was perfectly content.

And then I met Lynn, and my world split wide open.

4

AWAKENING

WORKING AT THE WORCESTER YMCA, I developed a new circle of friends thanks to my friend Jeanne, the aquatics director. They were strong, accomplished women who were comfortable in their skin. Jeanne introduced me to her friend Lynn, who shared my passion for sports and lived just up the street from me. Lynn Oski quickly became one of my closest friends. She was easy to talk to, funny, and whip-smart, and she had an upbeat personality that was infectious. She had a female life partner, and together they broke the hackneyed stereotype of gay women, presenting a much more relatable, feminine image. Lynn possessed the courage to follow her heart and live life on her own terms, and she had found great success both personally and professionally as a doctor.

One day Lynn told me she was going to race a triathlon and invited me to come watch.

"Yeah, sure, sounds fun!" I replied enthusiastically, without any inkling what a triathlon was. I'd never even heard the word before. I knew Lynn was into Jet Skiing, and the race took place at a nearby lake, so I concluded it was probably related to that.

The following weekend, I turned up to cheer on my friend in her mystery challenge. I stood on the sidelines and watched all kinds of people—a wide swath of ages and sizes—as they first charged into the lake and swam to a marked buoy and back to shore, then got on their waiting bicycles to ride a loop as fast as they could, *and then* went for a run. These people were pushing themselves to their physical limits, yet they all seemed to be somehow enjoying it, flashing quick smiles at us cheering on the sidelines and just looking so . . . proud. I was fascinated. When I met Lynn at the finish line, I just about tackled her.

"Oh, my God, Lynn!" I exclaimed, the words falling out excitedly, breathlessly. "This is the coolest thing I've ever seen!"

She just looked at me, smiling and chuckling, still trying to catch her own breath.

Everyone seemed equally fired up as they approached the finish line. They were ordinary people rising to an extraordinary challenge and having a damn good time doing it. They looked totally spent but *happy*. As I sat with Lynn and her triathlete friends around our picnic lunch listening to their animated race replays, one thought kept surfacing in my mind: *I have to do this.*

Back home, I could not wait to become a triathlete in training. There was just one small hitch: I had no idea where to begin. Sure, I was a certified personal trainer who had no problem prescribing a get-fit program to Y clients, but I had zero clue how to approach triathlon or endurance training. I asked Lynn if she'd mind if I tagged along on some training sessions. My eagerness coupled with her supportive nature made it impossible for her to say no. We'd meet at the hospital where she worked as a sleep-disorders researcher and go for a 30-minute jog that would absolutely destroy me. Lynn was in great shape—she was winning her age group in local races. The extent of my running had always been short, explosive sprints down the field for field hockey and lacrosse. Race to the ball. Flick the ball. Run back into position. In college, a big run training day was a mile warm-up followed by a dozen line sprints—that was it. When I started running with Lynn, I could maintain the pace for the short warm-up but really struggled to keep up after that. But Lynn never made me feel self-conscious about the chasm between our actual endurance capacities. I'd be loudly huffing and puffing, and she'd stop midrun to point out a random sight, saying, "Check out that cool house!" or "Hey, look at those grazing cows!" She had to know I was about to collapse. But instead of feeling deflated after these runs, I was determined to get stronger for our next run.

Because I idolized Lynn, it was inevitable that I'd develop an enormous crush on her. But I respected the fact that she was in a wonderful relationship, and I was content to have this incredible role model as one of my best friends. My feelings for Lynn gave me further confidence that it was women, not men, who brought out the best in me and gave me butterflies in my belly.

When Lynn asked me if I knew how to swim, I shrugged off her question with a cool "Yeah, I can swim." We went to the local Bally health club, which had a 15-yard pool, for my first swim workout. Swimming, to me, had been games of Marco Polo and dead man's float as a kid. As I stood on the pool deck watching people swim up and down the length of the pool, I tried to absorb as many visual cues as I could in a mash-up crash course on freestyle stroke mechanics. When it came time to take the plunge, I "swam" the way my mom did when she didn't want to get her hair wet. We called her "the Swan" for good reason. With my neck craned forward, I was trying so hard to propel myself that my arms and legs were left to spastically thrash around, creating a counterproductive whirlpool effect. I barely made it across the pool.

Luckily, Lynn didn't flee the pool deck after that first lap. She patiently taught me how to swim with my entire head in the water (terrifying) and how to breathe (without stopping midstroke!). She showed me some swim drills to help me develop proper technique. I felt perpetually guilty because I knew she only had an hour lunch break to squeeze in her own swim workout, and she spent most of it trying to help me not drown. But with her help, I was able to swim a few laps and worked my way up to 1,500 yards within a few weeks. Every single day I went to the pool and swam 1,500 yards. It took my entire 45-minute lunch break.

A few months after I started swimming, Lynn invited me to join a proper swim session at a nearby 25-yard pool. I was so psyched that I got there an hour early. But my excitement turned to frustration minutes into the warm-up as I started getting lapped. A lot. I felt that I was just getting in everyone's way and being an annoyance. I moved to the other end of the pool, feeling defeated.

Surely the cycling had to come easier. At that point in my life—I was 24—childhood joy rides were the extent of my cycling experience. My yellow bicycle with a banana seat and pink streamers had been my pride and joy, and I had spent hours riding it up and down our dead-end street. But one day, during a spat with Lisa, she threw it into a creek, and I watched in horror as it floated away from me. The only other time I had been on a bike was when we visited Fire Island in New York each summer and I borrowed my aunt's rusty cruiser to ride down the boardwalk to the ice-cream shop.

Lynn told me her neighbor was selling his 10-speed bike for $100. That sounded like an awful lot of money, but I decided to check it out. The bike was electric blue and had a front basket and these clever straps over the pedals to hold your feet in place. I was especially psyched about the basket so I could carry my stereo and ride with music. I bought the bike and started riding 35 minutes to an hour every day, per Lynn's instruction. I'd pedal the same route to a nearby lake and back.

Soon I was averaging 18 miles per hour on my rides. It was hard, but I was relieved that my innate cycling strength might help make up for my lackluster swimming and running. On the bike I felt strong, fast, and confident. Still, I couldn't help noticing that I wasn't the strongest cyclist on the road. Not by a stretch. I was getting dropped by teenagers on beach cruisers and thick guys on mountain bikes. It was puzzling.

I told Lynn how humbled and impressed I was by the cycling talent in our area. Here I was nearly pushing 20 mph and getting dropped right and left.

"Are you sure your speedometer is working correctly?" Lynn asked earnestly, walking over to my bike to investigate.

"Yeah, I just had it fixed—it works perfectly," I said, watching her lift my bike and spin the rear wheel, then lean in to see the reading.

"Siri, this speedometer is set to read kilometers per hour, not miles," she said, laughing off my mistake.

All that time I was going maybe 11 miles per hour. The realization brought me crashing back to earth. I had my work cut out for me.

In a storyline that was beginning to feel all too familiar, I perpetually felt intimidated and guilty on group rides because either people would have to wait for me, or I was holding them back. Every time I showed up for a ride, I believed every single rider who saw me was thinking, "Oh, great, here comes Siri." I desperately wanted to change that perception.

In addition to a weekend group "long ride" of about an hour and a half, Lynn and I would train on the Lifecycle stationary bikes at Bally. I began doing most of my harder bike sessions indoors. We'd meet at the gym at 5 a.m. for interval workouts, which Lynn would guide. Our hour-long session would be a series of 3 minutes hard, 2 minutes easy, 5 minutes hard, 1 minute easy, with changes in resistance.

During this time I began having the same recurring dream. I am standing in a sea of people—thousands of people. Every person is trying to say something, but I can't hear anyone's words clearly; it's just a cacophony of sound. But then I lift my head above the others and start speaking, and my voice transcends the din. My speech rings out with clarity and force, and at the sound of it my heart is so full it could burst. After spending so many years of my youth feeling powerless, triathlon training fed my deepest yearnings. I wanted to see what I was capable of on my own. My previous athletic experience in team sports left me to wonder how much of my success could be attributed to me. If I could achieve something special independently, it would validate all that I'd accomplished in my team sports. It would prove that I'd mattered. Nothing was going to stop me from improving, from being a legitimate swimmer, cyclist, and runner—a triathlete.

By the end of the summer, Lynn and I felt my training was at a point where I could enter a race. I was swimming 35 minutes somewhat continuously three or four times per week. I was feeling stronger on the bike. And I'd slowly built up to running five days a week, with my longest run lasting an hour. I'd also started doing some strength training in the gym.

I had one nonnegotiable requirement for my first race: absolute anonymity. There was no way I was going to attempt this feat in front of Lynn or my friends. I didn't need any outside pressure in addition to my mounting anxiety about the race itself. So I decided to fly to Colorado to race. My mom was living in Vail, and her unconditional support helped to calm my nerves. The day before the race, I bought a new bathing suit and rented a 10-speed from the local bike shop—all the lighter bikes had been rented, so I was fitted with a steel beast.

The sprint race (800-meter swim, 12-mile ride, and 3.1-mile run) was in the Denver suburb of Englewood. The night before the race, I stuffed myself with pasta, bread, chicken, and cookies. I felt like I was going to burst but kept eating.

"Are you sure you're supposed to eat that much?" asked M, unable to mask the trace of concern in her voice.

"Mom. Yeah, it's called carbo-loading," I said matter-of-factly. I had this race nutrition thing dialed.

I couldn't sleep at all that night—endorphins were coursing through my body, and I kept getting up to pee. When the alarm sounded, I leaped out of bed, still full and totally amped for race day.

When we arrived at the race site, the local YMCA, the registration volunteer asked me for my 100-yard pace so she could assign me to the appropriate start wave for the pool swim. I looked at her blankly. I'd never timed myself over 100 yards and had no idea what to tell her.

"Sorry, I'm not really sure?" I stammered, noticing the line behind me growing longer with antsy racers.

"Is it 2 minutes? One forty? One twenty?" she asked, her patience starting to wane.

"Honestly, I don't know," I said sheepishly.

"Well, what's your best guess, then?" She was over it.

"One twenty?" I blurted. It was a total stab in the dark.

"Okay, you're in lane 3 and start at 8:15—don't be late," she said, already looking to the next athlete in line.

Fifteen minutes before my start time, I walked over to my assigned lane. Five other people—all guys—stood at the end of lane 3. They were lean and muscular, with triangular chests and broad shoulders. They looked like, well, swimmers. I felt sick to my stomach. But then I remembered Lynn telling me that sometimes the ones who look the fittest aren't always the fastest. What mattered was how efficient you were in the water.

Waiting for the race to start, I thought I might come out of my skin—or pass out. Maybe both.

Someone on a megaphone blew a horn, and we were under way. For 10 minutes straight, I got absolutely pummeled. I was swimming at a pace of maybe 2 minutes per 100 yards (and most certainly not in a straight line), while the guys in my lane were moving at sub-1:20 speed. But I didn't slow or stop to let anyone pass, and they were forced to swim over or around me. It felt like being mauled inside an active washing machine. The guys were visibly annoyed by this rogue intruder, as were the race organizers on deck, but I was too focused on my own race to really care. Finally, the guys in my lane got out and left me to finish the last half of my swim in calmer water.

When I completed the 750 meters, I crawled out of the pool totally flustered but exhilarated. M was frantically waving her arms and shouting, "Siri! Siri! Over here! I've got your shorts!" I was nearly hyperventilating when I reached her (I hadn't considered the added challenge of the mile-high altitude). She held out my Spandex shorts for me to step into, but as I wrestled to get them up over my wet legs I lost my balance and tipped over, shrieking. M knelt down and was trying to help me get my other leg into the shorts when a referee ran over, shouting, "Hey! You can't give outside assistance! She will get disqualified!" Mom, verging on tears, told the referee, "But this is my daughter!"

We were making the biggest scene.

I finally got my shorts on and went charging off toward my bike. Because of the multiple-wave start, there were still a number of bikes in transition, which gave me a confidence boost. I was still ahead of all those people. The 20-kilometer bike course consisted of five laps. Five excruciating, Mt. Everest–scale laps. (When I went back to that area years later, I noted that the bike course was actually gently rolling at most.) I pushed those pedals with all I had and still got passed and lapped as if I were soft-pedaling to Sunday brunch. I felt like everyone was snickering at my snail's pace as they dropped me in commanding style.

Deflated but not wholly discouraged, I finally arrived back to transition. M was there to receive me, cheering like I was gunning for Olympic gold. I was happy to be off my bike and excited to tackle the 5K run. I sprinted out of transition on wonky legs like a bat out of hell. About 100 meters later, I had to stop and bend over, gasping for air and on the verge of throwing up. I composed myself and took off again in a sprint, only to stop in another 100 meters to repeat the same gasp-and-gag routine. I ran the entire 5K like that. It never occurred to me that if I slowed to a sustainable pace, I'd actually finish faster.

I reached the finish line ready to drop. M, with fat tears rolling down her cheeks, drew me into a huge hug. I'd done it. It had been agony from beginning to end, but I'd never felt more alive.

I grabbed some orange slices, water, and a Power Bar and let it all sink in. Walking back to transition together, Mom asked me if I wanted to get lunch to celebrate. I looked at her in disbelief. "Mom, the awards are in an hour!" In a compassionate gesture, she agreed to go. She knew I had finished nearly dead last.

That night, lying in bed, I started replaying the race in my mind, except this time I was seeing myself through the eyes of the other racers. Images I had clearly registered but blocked out until then flooded cruelly into view as if I had turned on the TV. I cringed at what I saw: flashes of faces expressing shock or pity at my attempt to become a triathlete. A wave of deep embarrassment came crashing down on me, and I felt like a cross between an impostor and an utter flop. I started bawling.

I ran into my mom's bedroom, hot tears streaming down my cheeks.

"That was such a disaster; I feel so humiliated!" I cried, crumbling onto her bed.

"Siri, you're *so* good at so many other things," M reasoned.

"But I want this more than anything in the world! This is all that matters to me," I sobbed, inconsolable.

"Okay, honey," she soothed. "I will support you in this for two years, but if in two years it's not working out, promise me you'll go and do something else."

But it wasn't a question of *if* it would work out—it was a matter of *when*. I had suffered physically and mentally as never before in my life, and I had loved every minute of it. I was as hungry as I was humbled.

The fire had been lit.

5

DESTINY

I WENT BACK TO MASSACHUSETTS and told Lynn I wanted to throw myself into training. I was working 60-hour weeks at the Y, so I would wake up at 4 a.m. and ride or run, work a few hours, try to get in a swim at lunch and another session after work, then go to bed reasonably early so I could get up and do it all again the next day. I was training as if I were a professional triathlete, but I was painfully slow.

About six months into my training, in March 1994, Lynn took me to get a bike at Landry's Cycle Shop in Worcester, Massachusetts. It was a Cannondale R700 with 650 wheels. The shop also threw in a bike jersey with its logo, and wearing it on my new steed, I felt like a million bucks. The bike was light and fast and had a few more gears than my old one. The new bike and Landry's "sponsorship" gave me motivation, and I felt that my training was a serious pursuit now. This setup was way too nice for me to suck as a cyclist. I couldn't just look the part—I had to *be* the part. I had to prove I was worthy of the real-deal equipment.

I bought a pair of Speedplay clipless pedals and corresponding cleats, and Lynn spent a week trying to teach me how to clip in and out of the pedals. She would steady my bike as I attempted to clip in and out, screeching and wobbling. We put my bike on the indoor trainer, and I practiced finding that sweet spot where the cleat snapped into the pedal and torquing my ankle just enough to release my shoe. When I felt decently confident, we ventured outdoors. The road we both lived on led to a main thoroughfare that connected to all the ride routes. There was a steep section, and I'd come barreling down the hill with a death squeeze on the brakes, panicked about having to clip out at the bottom. The more nervous I was, the more erratic and unstable I became. I fell more than a couple times, sometimes at a stoplight with drivers looking on in amusement. I would have a panic attack whenever I approached a stop sign, unsure whether I'd be able to clip out in time or whether I'd come tumbling off my bike in slow motion. Even when I was clipped in, I didn't trust that a pedal the size of a watch face would support my entire weight, so I pressed tentatively on the pedals for quite some time before I learned to trust them.

I was swimming and running six days a week and riding three to four days. I also lifted weights a few times a week. I jumped into a statewide race series to put all of my training to the test. The Fiske Racing Series events—I did about eight of them that summer—were casual, family-friendly sprints with very small fields. I began finishing on the podium, and then I won one. I found that I could make up some of the deficit from my weak swim on the bike and then put in a solid effort on the run.

The following season, the local paper did a story about me, declaring "YMCA fitness coordinator one of the best in triathlon." There was a large photo of an exuberant 25-year-old me running in baggy shorts and a YMCA tank. The attention was exciting, if a bit premature. I had won three small races in my second season, including the Ashland Lions Triathlon, where I qualified for age-group nationals in Columbia, Maryland.

"I love this more than anything," I was quoted as saying in the article. "This is the first time that I've ever been faced with a challenge that whatever happens is totally up to me. If I'm going to win, I have to push myself to the limit. If I don't win or I do terribly, it's totally my fault."

In triathlon, unlike in my high school sports, I felt that my success hinged solely on me. That notion was both daunting and exciting.

"My absolute dream would be to go to Nationals and do really well and have the opportunity to go to [age-group world's in] Wellington, New Zealand," I told the reporter.

I made the six-hour drive from Massachusetts to Maryland with my girlfriend, Kristy. We took my Jeep, which, unbeknownst to me at the time, had a carbon monoxide leak. I felt terrible during the race—lethargic with a dull headache—and finished a disappointing 13th. The top-12 finishers were invited to go to world's, and I just missed the cut. After arriving back home, my friend and I both paid a visit to the doctor and realized we had carbon monoxide poisoning. We had to be on oxygen for a couple of days to fully recover.

About three weeks later, I got a call from USA Triathlon (USAT), the sport's governing body. The 12th place finisher couldn't go to the world championships, and since I was 13th, the spot rolled down to me. I could not contain my initial excitement, and I told the caller that of course I was in—100 percent yes. But right after I hung up the phone, I started to feel like an impostor. The critical voice in my head said I hadn't been good enough to make the team outright, so I had no business going. I channeled that self-doubt, and it motivated me to want to learn more and train harder. I thought about nothing else but triathlon.

When I was prepping for Wellington, I went out for a ride one day with Lynn and her training group. I was dropped within five minutes, and that was an easy ride for them. After the ride, a guy named Charlie came up to me.

"Look, New Zealand is going to be a pretty hilly course, so before you go, you might want to work on your cycling because you are really going to suffer on that bike course," he said.

In Maryland, where I'd finished 13th, I had struggled on the hilly course. I'd never done any real hill training before. The area around Worcester had some small climbs, but you had to ride pretty far to get to them, and my rides would have been over before I even reached them.

Charlie, with some help from Lynn, wrote a cycling program for me. They had me train on a hilly loop near my house. I'd go hard up one hill and then go easy and recover until I got to the next hill, and then I'd go hard again. It was basic but effective. Riding had always been hard, but now I knew the real definition of *hard*. I still did my Bally interval rides with Lynn, and between the interval work and the hills program, my cycling started to improve.

My YMCA family was incredibly supportive. I couldn't afford the trip to New Zealand, so my coworkers hosted a fund-raiser in the rec room with pizza, soda, and a variety of homemade baked goods. I'm still not sure how it was arranged, but the governor of Massachusetts, William Weld, even showed up. He presented me with a congratulatory certificate for making the age-group triathlete world championship team. By the end of the night, I had the $2,500 I needed. I was humbled by all of the people who came together to support my triathlon ambition when I could count the number of races I'd done on two hands. I think they believed in me because they could see how enthusiastic I was to become better at it. They gave me an added incentive to do well, and I felt a big responsibility to not let them down. They thought I could be successful in this sport, and I just had to prove it to myself.

I met Uncle Boyce and Aunt Karen in Boston for the Head of the Charles Regatta—my cousin Michael was rowing in it. At lunch, Uncle Boyce presented me with a check for $500 that the whole family had pitched in for. He made a big deal of presenting it to me and delivered a short, poignant speech. He said he knew I was capable of doing something special even though I was new to the sport. I'd always had that raw potential, he said, and he was pleased that I'd found my passion. Uncle Boyce always had a way of making me feel special—I was again that little kid sitting on his deck on

Fire Island, basking in his praise and buoyed by his assurance that I could be extraordinary.

In November, it was time to head to New Zealand. To get my bike there, I had to take it apart and pack it in my spiffy new Tri All 3 hard-shell bike case. I had zero clue how to break down my bike, and after working at it for three frustrating hours, I ended up putting the whole tangle of parts in my car and driving to Landry's, where I paid to have my bike properly packed.

When I got to New Zealand, I frantically sought out a mechanic to put my bike together for me. I found one right in town, and he assembled my bike, except he didn't put on my pedals because I'd accidentally left them in my suitcase. He talked me through how to screw them on and gave me the necessary tool. It took me about an hour to get both pedals back on my bike, but I was just relieved to have gotten the job done.

The next morning, I met up with the team to go for a spin to do a little course recon and shake the residual jet lag from our legs. I was riding blissfully along, soaking in the sights and feeling grateful for this incredible opportunity, when one of my pedals popped right off the crank. Instinctively, I stuck my leg (with the pedal still affixed to my shoe) straight out, quickly becoming off-kilter. I started to panic, and teetered over. It felt like a bad dream.

On race day, I survived the swim, hammered the hills to the best of my (improved) ability, and managed to run my way through much of the field. I ended up placing seventh in my 25–29 age group (and as the second American woman). I'd really stepped up my training for world's and thought that if I kept elevating my game and making small but hard-fought gains, maybe I could do something significant in this sport. The glimmer of a dream was gathering embers: *Someday, I could be great.*

A couple of months later, I flew out to Colorado to be with my mom for the holidays. She was living in Vail, and I'd rarely visited her because I loved the East Coast, and now I couldn't tear myself away from my training. After she picked me up at the Denver airport, she said she had to make a quick stop in Boulder to run an errand. I grumbled about it since the detour would add to our three-hour drive home. But she insisted it was important. An hour later, we pulled up to the Boulder Reservoir. It was a beautiful, sunny day—unseasonably mild and not what I expected of winter in Colorado. There were even a few sailboats on the water and dozens of people riding and running around the reservoir. I couldn't believe this was a real place—I was fascinated and immediately enamored. Compared to Worcester, where there were few bike lanes, way too much traffic on the roads to ever feel safe, and extreme New England weather, this seemed like the ideal place to swim, bike, and run in the great outdoors.

My mom knew I was in love with triathlon and that once I saw Boulder, I'd want to move there, and she'd have me nearby. She parked the car facing the water and got out, saying she'd be right back. She simply walked until she was out of my sight and waited for 10 minutes as I took in the whole scene.

"Oh, my God, this place is unreal—did you see all those runners and cyclists?" I said, beaming, when she returned to the car.

"Yeah, I guess it's a popular training spot for triathletes," she said casually.

We headed into town for lunch. She took me out for sushi, my favorite, and then we swung by the Pearl Street Mall and strolled the stores together. It was a happy afternoon filled with all the things I loved.

In Vail the next day, I decided to go cross-country skiing. It was a beautiful bluebird day on the snow-blanketed golf course bisected by freshly groomed Nordic tracks. As I approached the end of a trail, I noticed a group of six or seven women doing a snowshoe relay race. I stared a moment too long, losing my focus—and then my balance. My skis slid out from beneath me, and I tumbled to the ground, hitting my butt hard, my skis splaying out in opposite directions.

A woman from the group—a fit-looking Latina with short black hair—came running over.

"Are you okay? That was a good spill!"

"Oh, yeah, I'm all right—I'm just new to this," I said as casually as I could, eyes pointing down. My pride hurt way more than my aching backside.

"Ah, don't worry about it—I'm just starting out, too," she replied. Her high energy seemed boundless.

"Where are you from?" she asked, filling the silence as I struggled back to my feet.

"Massachusetts. I'm here for a week visiting my mom. How about you?" My breath was fast as I finally found my footing.

"I live in Boulder," she said, the trace of a native Spanish speaker's accent in her voice.

"Oh, no way! I was just there yesterday," I said excitedly.

"That's my team," she said, pointing to the group of women. "I'm their coach."

"Oh, cool, what do you coach?" I asked.

"Triathlon," she said.

She began to speak again, undoubtedly preparing to explain what a triathlon was, but I cut her off.

"Are you kidding me?" I said, feeling immediately like kinfolk. "I just started doing triathlon, and I'm totally in love with it. It's what I want to do."

Her name was Yoli Casas. Every year she brought her athletes to Vail for some winter high-altitude training. When she introduced me to her girlfriend, Sasha, I realized that Yoli was also proudly gay. Standing in my ski boots on that frozen golf course, I told her all about my training with Lynn and recent races, absent the most embarrassing details. I'd humiliated myself in front of this woman enough for one day.

"If you're really serious about triathlon training, Boulder is the place to be," she said. "One of my athletes, Gloria, is looking to rent out a room, and if you're interested, I can introduce you to her—she's standing right over there."

Gloria, who had the same warm, cheery disposition as Yoli, explained that she'd just bought a house in North Boulder that was close to a pool, running trails, and ride routes and that she was looking for someone to cover $50 per week.

Yoli chimed in.

"And if you'd consider it, I'd be happy to give you some coaching guidance, and you can just pay me what you can—and then when you get a job, you can pay me a little more."

Kismet, fate, grace, luck, whatever you call it—I couldn't believe this was all happening.

I rushed back to M's condo, feeling like I could burst in anticipation.

"Mom, you won't believe what just happened to me," I said, dropping my gear at the door and unzipping my jacket as I searched out M, whom I found in the kitchen dicing tomatoes.

The words came tumbling out as I described my encounter. The serendipity was not lost on M, who was equally excited for me. We didn't even discuss the decision of uprooting my life in Massachusetts—the assumption was that I had to jump at this incredible opportunity that had just fallen into my lap. It was simply a matter of logistics.

I flew back home and gave notice at my job. Everyone at the Y was unbelievably understanding and genuinely happy for me. They'd supported my New Zealand trip, and this seemed like the natural next step in my triathlon pursuit. I couldn't wait to leave for Boulder. I packed one bag and my bike and flew to Colorado two weeks later, in February 1995. A friend sold the rest of my stuff in a yard sale after I left.

Yoli wasn't sure I'd really follow through on her offer—clearly she was just getting introduced to my zeal. I didn't doubt for a second that I'd made the right choice in moving to Boulder. It seemed that everything had conspired for me to be right where I was supposed to be. I was ready to give myself over to this new challenge, body and soul.

My first run workout with Yoli was at North Boulder Park. I couldn't wait. I had been nursing a knee strain right before the move and had been taking it easy and looking after it carefully, so I felt eager to get my new run program under way with my new coach. Yoli and I started to run at a fairly easy pace, maybe 9:30 per mile, and five minutes later, she slowed to a stop.

"Okay, that's good for today," she said.

"What? That's it?" I asked, confused.

"Look, Siri, you're just getting over an injury, so we are going to bring you back slowly. Be smart about it. Not rush things."

Every day we built on that first run until I was 100 percent healthy.

That early encounter exemplified what was so effective about Yoli, a former professional runner and triathlete from Venezuela who had earned an exercise physiology degree. She was incredibly methodical and patient with my training progression. She trusted the process. Yoli was full of passion and energy, but she never gave me too much training load or intensity too soon, and she tempered my gusto when I needed it.

Yoli told me to go to her friend Jane Scott's swim workouts. I had never heard of masters workouts, and she explained that Jane oversaw the popular Boulder Aquatic Masters swim club. She said Jane would teach me how to swim properly and help me get faster. She was also the sister of Dave Scott, the six-time Ironman® world champion.

I showed up at masters one early spring morning to ask Jane to work with me. When she asked about my goals, I answered without a moment's hesitation, "I want to learn how to swim—fast."

"I can help you, but you need to commit to coming five days per week," she said.

Done. I was ready to get started then and there.

Jane put me in a lane with a few other people who had already finished the warm-up while we'd been chatting. She gave out the first set—10 50s on 1 minute. I started laughing.

"Ha! That's the funniest thing I've ever heard—like we're going to do 20 laps in a minute. Ha ha!"

I thought it must be some kind of prank or hazing ritual for new swimmers. *Let's see if we can scare off the new girl in the first minute.* Everybody was staring at me.

Jane turned to me and explained, "You only have to go up and back in a minute, 10 times through."

Oh. I could feel my cheeks getting hot.

I struggled to make the 1-minute interval. From there on out, it was always touch the wall and go. And that was for the very "easiest" sets.

In addition to the basics of swim mechanics, technique, and training protocol, Jane taught me, after numerous attempts, how to do a flip turn. She was exceedingly patient but also tough. She would always put me with a strong swimmer named Kim and tell me to try to keep on Kim's feet as long as I could. If I fell back, I just needed to wait on the wall for her and then take off again in her draft. This game of cat-and-mouse with a much faster swimmer was incredibly frustrating.

"Why am I in this lane? I don't belong here," I'd complain to Jane.

"Siri, if you want to get faster, you've got to know what fast feels like and try to hang on as long as you can," she'd reason.

The experience forced me to accept the fact that in order to see real gains, I was going to get beaten up. A lot. I was going to feel like crap both physically and mentally, but I needed to learn to be resilient and not let the frustration discourage me from pushing through the discomfort.

I kept at it, worked hard, cried sometimes, and started to see my times drop. I went from a 32-minute 1,500 to 25 minutes. Seeing progress kept me motivated and hungry. I just needed to keep putting in the training and not get disheartened. There was a lot of room for improvement so long as I was willing to work for it.

The transition from the basic beginner's program that Lynn gave me to Yoli's long-term plan that incorporated aerobic build, strength, and speed phases was eye-opening. Yoli designed some workouts to build my endurance while others developed speed or strength. I could see and feel that I was becoming a more complete athlete. She also taught me about transitions and the importance of having a strong mental game. Most importantly, Yoli encouraged me to never lose sight of why I was doing this sport in the first place—for the love and enjoyment of it. Her positive attitude and vivacious energy were infectious, and she imprinted on me the conviction that I could work my butt off to get the very best out of myself while never losing perspective. She was invested in my progression as an athlete, but she was equally committed to helping me be a grounded, conscientious person so that win or lose, I could take pride in myself. She gave me an appreciation that sport was ultimately supposed to enrich my life, not consume it. Yoli taught me to train with gratitude.

I paid her next to nothing to train me, and she still treated me like I was a top priority. She told me to somehow pay it forward in the future. I barely paid the bills with my job teaching spin classes at a local gym called RallySport, where I also worked in the deli making sandwiches. At the end of the day, I'd put leftover bagels in my bag, assuming they'd probably just be tossed out anyway. One day the owners called me into their office and said they'd caught me on surveillance video taking food. I thought I was going to get arrested, but instead they told me that all I had to do was ask if I needed help.

Underneath my passion for the sport of triathlon, I had an internal drive that was irrepressible. Every time I tackled a key workout, I expected to do it better than the last time. If I didn't, or if it was worse, I'd be furious with myself. I had to see a forward progression. There were disappointing performances and plenty of moments when it felt like I was in a backslide. Yoli shifted my impatient, short-sighted perspective to the bigger picture. Over time I began to get the self-critiques under control. In the face of a subpar result, I had to learn how to resist the urge to discount myself as a hack triathlete. It was just a bad day.

Yoli also knew how far she could push me—she was like a silent assassin—and she coaxed out my alter ego with really painful workouts. Every week we did 8 × 400s on the track. I'd be pushing with absolutely everything I had, my legs and lungs screaming in protest. Yoli would be on the sideline cheering, "You look great, Siri!" and I'd say, "Fuck you, Yoli!" without breaking stride as I passed her. I knew that if I didn't give my absolute best, I'd never forgive myself, and I was pissed that killing myself on that track was my only option. I knew that if I let up at all, it would be the beginning of the end for me. Yoli always let it roll off her back, often in amusement at my over-the-top intensity.

Yoli knew better than anyone that I was strong willed to the point of being exasperatingly stubborn. One story illustrates this hallmark trait. There is a popular but very difficult 67-mile bike loop that goes from Boulder to the high-mountain town of Ward and back. I'd never done a ride longer than 90 minutes when I joined Yoli's group, and I was excited when the weekend training plans called for this epic ride. But about an hour after we began, a fast-moving storm rolled in, and it started to snow. The wind was whipping, and we were all soon frozen to the bone. Yoli, who would always follow her athletes on rides in her SUV, had everyone stop riding and pile into her car for the drive back to Boulder. Everyone was relieved to cut the ride short and retreat into the warmth and safety of her car. But I kept riding. Yoli pulled up to me and shouted out the window, "Okay, Siri, time to get in—it's too cold and getting dangerous."

"No! I'm not getting in the car—I'm going the whole way!" I protested, eyes straight on the road ahead. But she wouldn't stop following and asking me to get in the car. When I got to Ward, I stuffed newspapers down my jersey for insulation and got back on my bike. She could see that I was undeterred whatever the obstacle or degree of hardship. I couldn't reveal a chink in the armor for fear of the whole protective shield falling apart.

When I came to Yoli, I didn't understand the more technical nuances of riding. She explained things like cadence, pedal-stroke efficiency, and gearing. She gave me homework to help me learn how my gearing worked. She had me ride often with a German pro triathlete named Kerstin Weule, and I benefited a lot from riding with a stronger, more experienced cyclist. Yoli would send me off on group rides, and sometimes I'd come back to her 15 minutes later in tears after getting dropped. But then I was coming back 30 minutes after the start of those rides, then maybe 45 minutes later, until one day I didn't come back until the end of the ride. That was a good day.

Yoli would come to all of my races with me, road tripping as far as Tennessee if she had to, and she pushed me to be not only a better athlete but, more importantly, a better person. She would put me in my place when I needed it. Once when I complained about having to do a ride with someone who was slower than I, she said, "You're going to ride with this person, and you're going to be gracious about it—end of story." She helped me develop a firm sense of who I wanted to be as a person—my character, values, and priorities—when I started finding more success in the sport. Yoli both grounded me and let me soar.

I wanted to turn pro in 1995, but Yoli said the day I won the age-group national championship was the day I could go pro. My triathlon idol at the time was American pro Karen Smyers, who had won the 1990 International Triathlon Union (ITU) world title and was still dominating the pro ranks, and a chance encounter with her at the 1995 ITU World Championship in Cancún was pivotal in my decision to make the leap to pro. I'd gone to Cancún to compete in the age-group race—the ITU crowns world champions each year for elite pro triathletes, junior pro triathletes, and age-group athletes (in five-year age groups)—and finished third, while Karen won her second world title. After the race, I went to the beach and saw Karen relaxing with a beer. After I sheepishly introduced myself and told her she was my hero, she asked how I'd done in my race. When I told her I'd finished third, she sweetly congratulated me and asked if I'd ever thought about going pro. I told her the plan was to first win the national age-group title—and maybe even the world title—and then I would know I was ready.

"Don't be ridiculous," she said. "If you go as well as you did today, you will be fine. And even though you may not be at the same level as the pros right now, racing against them is going to lift your game. I really think you should take the chance."

This triathlon luminary telling me to turn pro was all the permission I needed. As an age-group triathlete, I always wanted to race in highly competitive fields with women who were capable of kicking my ass so I could measure myself against them. They gave me a standard to strive for and motivated me to train harder and smarter. The move to professional would take this peer inspiration to new heights. Yoli gave me her blessing (I was outkicked at the 1995 age-group national championship and came within seconds of winning), and M was also incredibly supportive.

In February 1996, we flew to Chile for my first pro race—the Pucón International Triathlon, an "Olympic"-distance event (the standard format of ITU racing: 1.5-km swim, 40-km bike, 10-km run). I felt like I had to prove I deserved to hold a pro card—the pressure was on. I ended up winning, which was hugely validating. At my next race, St. Anthony's in Florida, I finished seventh but ahead of other pro rookies like Jill Newman. Then we went to St. Croix, where I had some mechanical issues on the bike and finished a disappointing 13th, but I rebounded with a win at the Memphis in May Triathlon. I felt like I was on the right track.

In the beginning of my pro career, I was incredibly superstitious. My mom gave me a necklace that I wore all the time—it was a dolphin and a cross—and I'd kiss it for good luck before a race start. I'd do the same race-week workouts and eat the same pre-race meals (steak on Friday night, pasta with chicken, veggies, and red sauce the night before the race) and go through the race-morning ritual of reading the same motivational messages (which included excerpts from Jim Loehr's book *Mental Toughness Training for Sports*) and looking at photos of my dog Whoopi and cat Gertie back home as well as my old lacrosse coach Renee Spellman. Jane Scott had given me a small wooden horse figurine and told me to rub it for good luck, and I brought it to all my races. The superstitions and rituals (residual traces of my OCD) brought me some comfort and helped alleviate a bit of the pressure. I was still learning that true confidence and performance would come from putting in the training and nurturing my self-belief, not from stroking the miniature wooden horse in my pocket.

Yoli encouraged me to focus my career on ITU racing, which is a fast and furious format that permits drafting on the bike (as opposed to the majority of triathlons, including Ironman, where drafting will get you a time penalty or disqualified). The ability to draft lets you work with other riders to take turns blocking the wind at the front of a pack, or peloton. Developing a strong swim is especially essential in ITU racing because if you get left behind in the water and start the bike ride too far back in the field, the group dynamic (i.e., the drafting) on the bike can make it harder to reel in your competition. Racing ITU also demands a head-spinning amount of global travel to chase series points to qualify for the world championship. When it was created in 1991, the World Cup series consisted of 11 races in 8 countries. In 2009 the ITU also established the Dextro Energy Triathlon ITU World Championships Series (now the ITU World Triathlon Series), with 8 races in 8 countries. The prospect of traveling the world competing in the sport I loved *as my job* set my soul on fire.

My first ITU World Cup race was in Paris, France (I'd gone to Japan to do an ITU race, but we had ended up doing a duathlon because of a tsunami that hit right before the race), and I finished 18th but as the third American. Then I finished 16th at a World Cup race in Bermuda before coming back home to race Mrs. T's Chicago Triathlon, where I clocked the fastest run split by a pro woman and finished 11th. My swim was so weak that I could make it out with the second pack, but there was no way I could crack the top 10. Then I got a confidence boost from finishing 8th—and as the top rookie—at pro nationals that year.

I made it onto the ITU world championship team for Cleveland, Ohio. I remember being in an all-out sprint for 29th place. It wasn't the result I was hoping for, but I bounced back with a couple of top-five finishes at the French Grand Prix a month later. I finished out my rookie pro year with a 14th place finish at the ITU World Cup Finale in Noosa, Australia.

In 1997, I went down to New Zealand to train with two Kiwi triathletes, Jenny Rose, whom I'd met at my first ITU World Cup race in Paris, and Natasha Helgahold. Both Jenny and Natasha were coached by Jack Ralston, who was also working with Hamish Carter, the number-one triathlete in the world at the time. New Zealand and Australia, with its televised Formula One triathlon series, were hotbeds for triathlon and certainly seemed to offer greater opportunity than the States. (Even in Europe, the tri scene seemed more lively and professional than the one back home.) Jenny and I had started dating, and she took me under her wing and gave me an inside look at the level of commitment and work it took to win. I was jumping into some of their sessions while also still following Yoli's program, which created a training mash-up that would perturb any good coach. I really liked the workouts the others were doing because they were so challenging and different. And the squad was getting really good results. I was laser focused on advancing along the path that would help me become the triathlete I ultimately wanted to be, and Jenny was pivotal in helping me build momentum in the early trajectory of my career.

Later that season, I raced the world championship in Perth, where I finished 18th. I knew on the run that it would be impossible to crack the top 10, but I still sprinted like a medal was on the line. Minutes after my finish, a man approached me and said, "Congratulations, that was a really great effort."

"Thanks. Nice of you to say. I appreciate it," I replied.

"My name is Jack Ralston," he said. He had dark hair, a thick mustache, an athletic build, and a kind smile.

"Ah, yes, you coach Jenny, Natasha, and Hamish," I said, my breath still slowing.

"Listen, I've heard a lot about you, and if you ever want to try something different, I really believe that I can help you," he said. "I think you have a lot of potential, and I could be the person to take you to the next level."

He handed me a piece of paper with his phone number on it.

When I called him a few days later, I liked what he had to say. He had Yoli's enthusiasm but also the experience of coaching world-best triathletes.

I called Yoli the next day. I was a ball of nerves. The last thing I wanted was to come across as disloyal or ungrateful.

"Yoli," I started, "I can't thank you enough for all that you've done for me these past four years and how far we've come. You've helped me so much in so many ways, and there are no words to convey how grateful I am. It's just that I met this coach in New Zealand who works with some of the best triathletes in the world, and I really believe he can take what we've built up together and push things to the next level."

I braced for her reaction, my stomach in knots.

"Siri, that's wonderful," she said without hesitation. "Really. I think you should go for it. What a great opportunity. I think I've taught you everything I can, but I'm always going to be here to help you in whatever way you need."

Her unconditional support, understanding, and total lack of ego blew me away. She agreed that I was ready for the next step in my career and gave me her blessing to move on. I was moved to tears.

A couple of weeks later, I went to New Zealand for three months to dig into training with my new coach. Like Yoli, Jack told me to pay him whatever I could afford whenever I could afford it. He playfully said that winning the world championship would be his payment.

The training became much harder. Jack had me swimming with the whole New Zealand contingent. Most of them had been swimming their entire lives. Again, I was in way over my head and just trying to hang on. But the key to my improvement was not being afraid to put myself out there like bait in a sea of sharks and do the best I could to fend for myself and fight like hell. What was the worst that could happen? I could start to drown, but surely somebody would save me before it was too late. In New Zealand I swam with an open-water group every Tuesday night. We'd swim 1500 meters, and I'd get absolutely beaten to a pulp. But I kept remembering Jane's words: "If you want to swim faster, you have to swim with fast people. Just keep pushing forward." So that was what I did.

Jack made tweaks to my run form and cycling technique that helped me more fully maximize my ability. He shared his keen understanding of World Cup racing strategy and the unique mental battle it presented. He was always encouraging, and I drew confidence from his strong belief in me.

My relationship with Jenny was beginning to fizzle out, due mostly to the fact that my drive and passion for triathlon were all consuming, while her career was starting to wind down. She was satisfied with what she'd been able to achieve, while I was hungrier than ever.

When it was time to head back to Boulder for the remainder of the year (my schedule became three months in New Zealand, nine months back home in Boulder), Jack would communicate via fax and phone at the end of each week. The long-distance communication was tough. I was always a little nervous because I didn't know him as I knew Yoli and perceived him as a distant voice on the other side of the world. I missed the attentive, seamless interaction I'd shared with my old coach.

My main training partner in Boulder was a guy named Pat Brown. Also a fledgling pro, Pat had abundant positive energy and made training fun. He'd blast his "jock jams" CD to get us pumped up before a big workout or a race. I knew Pat was gay, and he knew I was gay, but we never acknowledged it. Still, the mutual understanding brought a deep comfort level to the friendship. Once we were both at a party and getting relentlessly teased because he didn't have a girlfriend and I didn't have a boyfriend, so we kissed each other just to get everyone to shut up. Years later, he told me he almost threw up while we were locking lips for show.

My other training partner, for my running at least, was my 80-pound terrier mix, Whoopi. The one constant in my life—the single source of support that has always sustained me—has always been my dogs, and Whoopi was much more than a pet. She was by my side on all my training runs. I would be tired before a run but when we hit the trail, her excitement inspired me. Her joy in the simple act of running and exploring was so freeing and fun that I started seeing the world as I envisioned her seeing it. That dog was a big reason that my run was becoming my weapon as a triathlete.

Six months after I started working with Jack, I flew to San Diego to race the 1998 USA Triathlon National Championship in Oceanside. Considering all the changes to my training, I didn't know what to expect. I caught a huge wave at the end of the swim and body-surfed my way toward the front, rode hard, and ended up running the fastest 10K of the day (34:20) to clinch the pro national title by nearly 1 minute. I was in total disbelief and ecstatic that I'd pulled off the win in a high-quality field that included stars like Barb Lindquist and Joanna Zeiger. Barb was a gutsy racer who never left anything on the racecourse. She was one of the first American women to venture abroad to race the Formula One series, beating the commanding Aussies on their own turf at their own game. Anything Barb did, I wanted to emulate. And Joanna was one of the best swimmers in the sport who excelled at long and short course.

After my Oceanside win, I landed my first sponsor, Ralph Lauren, which was looking to market its RLX activewear line through athlete sponsorships. A former Brown lacrosse teammate worked for the company, and she convinced them to take me on as an athlete with great potential. They also signed American Ironman athlete Tim DeBoom, who, like me, was still relatively unknown in the sport. I went to New York to meet with the company, and the guy I sat down with told me that Ralph Lauren was a family company and that I shouldn't let my training stand in the way of my having a *boy*friend. He also suggested I grow out my hair. He sent the message loud and clear: Tim and his beautiful athlete wife, Nicole, were a natural fit; I was not. The deal was lucrative, especially for that time in triathlon—they provided all my training equipment, including my Litespeed bike, wetsuit, clothes, shoes, and nutrition—and offered a generous bonus structure, agreeing to match prize money in the highly unlikely event of my winning a world title. With this sponsorship, I could focus solely on my training, which would propel me to the next level. That was all I wanted.

I invited a good guy friend of mine to training camp in Europe with the intent of dating him. "It was just a gay phase," I'd tell anyone who knew the real me. I felt like I had been shoved back in the closet and then slammed the door shut behind myself. I hated how untruthful it made me feel, and I didn't want to live a lie, but all that mattered was having these new means to pursue my triathlon dream and focus on my training like a real professional athlete. The results soon began to follow.

By the following year (1999), I was finishing in the top 10 in a lot of races and was ranked third in the World Cup standings. And although it was frustrating to be just out of podium reach, Jack was proud that I was consistently finishing fourth. He had come to the biggest race of the year, and he had been there for my very first top-10 World Cup finish (the previous year in Auckland, when I had finished seventh). "Consistency is a sign of a great athlete," he'd say.

Whenever I wanted M to come to one of my races, she'd be on the first plane out of Denver. She acted as my manager and became highly knowledgeable about the sport and the strengths and weaknesses of my closest competitors. She stood on the sidelines and cheered as my mom, but she was also a trusted adviser.

I had high hopes for the 1999 world championships in Montreal. I was confident in my preparation and had recorded personal bests in the swim, bike, and run. I'd been sleeping like a champ, eating perfectly, and weighed in at my ideal racing weight of 136 pounds. My dad and M were there as my top fans.

After a good swim and solid transition, I was right where I needed to be: in a bike pack with the past world champions Michellie Jones, Emma Carney, Jackie Gallagher and Joanne King. These women were the most dominant forces in the sport—it was surreal. The first corner came into view, and as I leaned my body into the turn and felt for a good line and balance point, the road beneath me gave out as if I'd cycled over a trapdoor. My front tire had peeled off the wheel, and I slammed onto the asphalt. On the ground, I was thinking, "Get up, Siri, you're still in this!" but as I was getting back on my feet, another cyclist came careening into me, and we both ended up in a tangle of bikes and limbs. My race was over.

One minute I was a perfectly peaked triathlete in the best possible position, and the next I was wallowing in DNF despair in the biggest race of my life. It seemed inexplicably random and unfair. As I sat crying and bleeding on the curb while photographers snapped my picture, someone sat down next to me. It was Sister Madonna Buder, a then 69-year-old triathlete and nun who has since become known as the Iron Nun (she is the oldest person to have ever finished an Ironman). She looked at me for a moment and then wrapped her arms around me in a hug. She quietly said a very warm and thoughtful prayer, which helped to calm me down and regain some perspective in that dark moment. I had two things to be grateful for: I hadn't been seriously injured, and with the Olympics just a year out, I'd exorcised the bad luck. That kind of misfortune when the stakes were highest surely wouldn't strike twice.

Despite the Montreal crash, I ended the 1999 season ranked fourth in the World Cup series and as the second-ranked American female triathlete in the world, behind Barb.

I started focusing on the 2000 Games, where triathlon would make its debut as an Olympic sport. I knew I had a solid shot at making Team USA as long as I continued to train well and execute the performance I knew I was capable of at the qualifier race.

Making the Olympic team soon became my singular goal. It absolutely consumed me.

6

TRIALS

THE TRIALS WERE TO BE HELD at the Olympic venue in Sydney, Australia. I decided I had to go to Sydney and live in solitude for the next seven months so I could devote myself to my mission, body and soul. Part of that decision was motivated by the disappointment—a subtle, abiding ache—surrounding my failed attempt at making the lacrosse national team. I would seize this special second chance to rewrite the ending to my original Olympic dream story (not counting the neighborhood games with the Polansky sisters). I had simply given up after not making the team, and I couldn't shake the feeling of deep shame. My response had made me feel weak and unmoored. Making Team USA would prove that I was tenacious, committed, and strong. It wouldn't change the fact that I had walked away from a sport I loved, but I'd make a meaningful statement: Siri Lindley is no quitter. I needed to prove to myself that I had the focus and determination to do it on my own, especially when things got hard. I didn't want any training partners or coaches to lean on or any distractions to erode my warrior-like discipline.

I rented a tiny apartment in Cronulla, a beach town in south Sydney known for its superb swimming facilities and running and cycling terrain. Except for my group swim workouts, I lived in total isolation. I ate all of my meals alone and told friends and family, including M, not to visit—not even for Christmas. (Mel Ashton, an Aussie triathlete, invited me to her family's Christmas dinner. For dessert, there was a cake with a coin buried inside it. Whoever got the coin was supposed to make a wish, which was destined to come true. I nearly choked on the coin, and in my panic I failed to make the obvious wish.) Living that kind of monastic life was completely contrary to my human nature, and I was intensely lonely and sorely missed my family, friends, and pets back home. But my support system wouldn't be on that start line with me; I needed to be fully self-reliant. I did my best to push the sadness out of my mind and harden myself. My Olympic dream took on the gravity of a spiritual quest.

It was as if everything I'd already accomplished in the sport didn't really matter—my absolute worth would be measured on Judgment Day, April 16, 2000. And I would know that I had done everything in my power to be the best I could be on that day. I would walk away with the confidence that I had given myself every chance to be successful.

Every night, before I drifted off to sleep in my altitude tent, I'd visualize the perfect race: a clean start with a great position in the swim, leading the first chase pack; a flawless transition and a strong and steady ride in the top five; another impeccable transition before starting the run still holding position in the front five; and finally a commanding, fast 10K, pushing myself to the absolute limit but with total confidence and no fear. It ended, of course, with me crossing the finish line as the first American and standing atop the podium in a flood of gratitude, exhilaration, and relief. *Triumph, flourish . . . and scene.*

If I fell asleep without finishing my visualization ritual, I'd startle awake in the middle of the night and start where I remembered leaving off. I approached this detailed mental rehearsal of my perfect race with as much discipline as I did my physical training.

On New Year's Day, I woke up at 4 a.m. and drove my trusty 1980 Mitsubishi Colt (which I'd bought for $400) into the center of Sydney. People filled the streets, champagne spilling from their plastic cups. I watched the sun come up over the Opera House, feeling inspired by the start of a new year ripe with opportunity. I thought it would be fun and personally meaningful to be the first person to run the Olympic triathlon course in the new century. I ran the two 5K laps skirting Sydney Harbor, dodging partyers who must've thought I was crazy. I envisioned myself on these same roads on an electric race day, imagining every sight, sound, and smell.

The local newspaper counted down the days until the Games on its front page, and my Olympic dream greeted me each morning upon waking. Just thinking about lining up at the start with the world's very best made my adrenaline rise. I could not wait for the day to give my absolute all and see how I measured up.

The day before the race, Jack and I went to the athlete meeting, after which I planned to ride the bike course. But when I got on my bike, I realized it wouldn't shift—it was totally locked up. I started to panic. Jack ran it over to the bike shop, and the mechanic on duty was able to troubleshoot the issue and delivered my bike to me at 9:30 that night. I told myself it didn't matter that I hadn't been able to ride the course one last time. I was ready.

On race morning, I was confident I'd prepared as well as I possibly could. I was in the best shape of my life, and now it was just a matter of executing the plan I'd rehearsed to a T in my head every night for the past 120 nights.

When I warmed up, my bike started out shifting normally, but then it started acting up again. A guy standing nearby took notice of my frenzied state and started fiddling with my bike. He got my gearing functioning again, and I just prayed it would cooperate during the race. I dropped the bike at my transition spot and headed for the start.

In a lineup 50 racers wide at the start, I tried to clear my head, relax, and refocus. I felt drained by the stress of dealing with my bike but did my best to stay loose and let it go. The gun went off, and we dove into Sydney Harbor. I was on the feet of Michellie Jones—the Aussie ITU superstar who was dominating the World Cup circuit—entering the first buoy turn when someone swam right over me, shoving me beneath the surface. Other racers continued to swim over me, and when I popped back up, choking for air, the lead pack had opened up a 2-meter gap. I panicked. That was not part of the plan. I'd never considered the need for a contingency strategy, and I was totally unprepared for the abrupt departure from my meticulous race rehearsal. I tried my hardest to sprint back to the group, but I couldn't close the gap. What felt like the most effortful swim of my life produced one of my slowest times.

Onto the bike, about 10 seconds from the chase pack, my legs were grinding away but I wasn't generating any power. I just had to ride hard and then run the way I knew I could, but I struggled to stay with riders I'd normally be pulling around on the racecourse. I was dropped from the third pack and then swallowed up by the fourth.

Onto the run, feeling totally demoralized and bewildered, I made it to the first kilometer and then spotted Jack. I decided right there and then to pull the plug.

"Are you sure you can't hold it together?" he pressed.

"I can't; I'm done," I said, tears rising in my throat.

The first thing I did was call M. She was hosting a party in Boulder with all my friends and following the race online.

When she picked up the phone, all she heard was my bawling.

"I don't know what happened—I had no strength from the very beginning," I explained between sobs.

I had choked. I'd put so much pressure on myself to have the perfect performance that I had set myself up to fail spectacularly. My fatal flaw was being so laser focused on a certain outcome that I couldn't adapt or respond to the race action as it was unfolding. The first American woman, Jennifer Gutierrez, claimed her spot on Team USA.

After the race, I fielded the same questions from journalists, friends, family, and other athletes over and over: "Were you sick?"

"Did you have an injury?" *"What happened?"* I had to answer that there was no reason except that I'd choked. I knew I had to own it if I was ever going to move on and keep it from happening again. I needed to stare it down head-on.

After Sydney, I'd lie in bed at night thinking about that race and fall into a seemingly bottomless emotional spiral. I felt trapped inside my body and mind and desperately wanted to run away from my thoughts, from myself. I didn't want to be this feeble person who had cracked—nay, detonated—under pressure.

This is not who I am.

Working through my emotions—and reflecting on the experience—I came to realize I had ventured off to Australia to access and nurture strengths that were already within me. I had the courage to go after my dream with total devotion and the discipline to prepare myself the best way I knew how. I was anything but a quitter.

I had to resort to Plan B, which was a second-round qualifying event in Dallas a few months later. I arrived four weeks early to prepare. Drawing some lessons from Sydney, I tried to avoid creating a pressure-cooker environment for myself. This time, my mom, dad, and old swim coach Jane Scott were there to support me. My training lead-in with Jack had gone smoothly, and I was sanguine.

In advance of Dallas, I wrote in a dispatch for *Triathlete* magazine, "The winning or the making of a national team will happen on its own, just as a result of my passionately performing out there with excitement and joy. This is what I forgot in Sydney. But now, heading into the Dallas Olympic Trials, I am reunited with all that makes me *me* and all that comprises this incredible passion I have for triathlon. I will go out there May 27th psyched to race, ready to accept the challenge, confident in my ability and secure in my thinking that I deserve to make the team."

On a scorching-hot race day, the swim went according to plan, and I rode at the front of the chase pack, doing a lot of the work. When I hit the run with fellow American Joanna Zeiger, she took off in pursuit of the two leaders, Barb Lindquist and Sheila Taormina, who had opened up a 4-minute lead. Historically, if I came off the bike with Joanna, I could shake her in the early stages of the run. But today offered a role reversal. It rattled me, and I started to feel the energy draining from my legs. Barb ended up collapsing from heat exhaustion (as she had in Sydney) before the finish line, and Sheila punched her Olympic ticket by finishing as the first American. The next finisher would earn the remaining spot. With 400 meters to go on the run, my vision started to blur, but I made it to the finish line before passing out. Volunteers rushed me to the medical tent, where they drained four intravenous fluid bags into me. Sheila and Joanna had made the Olympic team, and I would be an alternate. It was devastating to not qualify, but I still appreciated the opportunity to have the Olympic experience as part of Team USA.

But the next day, when the team was called together for a meeting, it was clear that the alternates were considered separate from the "real" Olympians. They divided us into two groups, and I felt lowly despite the fact that I was ranked higher in the World Cup series than the women who'd made the team outright.

After Dallas, I received an e-mail from an Australian pro triathlete named Loretta Harrop, whom I'd met the previous year when

I was racing on the Australian Grand Prix circuit, a fast and furious series of races around the country. We'd struck up a conversation during a bus ride from the hotel to the race venue and related easily to one another. I had told her about my Olympic dreams, which she, of course, also had for herself. We both approached racing like it was a dogfight, regardless of whether the podium was in sight. Loretta was the real deal—she'd won the 1999 ITU world championship in Montreal (where I'd crashed out) and finished the '99 season ranked number one in the World Cup series. I admired her.

"I know you must be going through a rough spot," she wrote. "You've got more in you, so don't give up." Loretta epitomized a tough-love mentality, and she wasn't one for flattery. Quite simply, she thought I needed "a little bit of a kick up the ass."

She said her coach—an Aussie named Brett Sutton who had coached multiple athletes to world titles—could help me, and she invited me to come to their training base in Switzerland. I was no stranger to the Sutton stigma, as stories of his forthright personality and brutal training loads were widely told, and he'd drawn some attention for an alleged inappropriate relationship with an athlete. "It will be the hardest thing you've ever done in your life," Loretta warned. "But I guarantee that you will get results. You will be twice the athlete you are today and you will prove to everybody that you should have been on that Olympic team. If nothing else, consider doing it for yourself."

I wrote her back, thanking her for the note and letting her know I'd consider the invitation. As flattered as I was, I was happy to be back in Boulder, surrounded by M, my friends, and my animals, after seven months in Australia. But after talking it over with M, I decided it was a rare opportunity that I couldn't pass up. I also talked to a few people who knew Brett, and they all spoke in support of him and dismissed the rumors and vilification. Since I hadn't made the Olympic team and my immediate plans had been upended, it was the perfect timing for a profound leap of faith. I wrote to Loretta again, telling her I was coming.

But Loretta hadn't spoken to Brett before extending the invitation to me, and when she did after receiving my response, he said, "No way. We're not having an American." He found Americans excessively talkative and generally cloying. Also, at 31, I was older, and he assumed I was already too set in my ways to be an apt pupil.

But Loretta persisted, telling him I'd be the sole American, with no choice but to fall into line. I had the makings of a real champion. Finally, he relented.

When Brett and I first talked on the phone, he told me he recalled seeing me at the 1996 world championship in Cleveland.

"I remember watching you sprinting all out for 29th place as if you were racing to win gold," he said. "That is what I look for in an athlete—a competitive fire to be your best, no matter your place. Good old-fashioned guts."

But he'd stopped taking notice of me because I was "too emotional to put it together in the main races, when it counted." With Loretta, one of his star athletes, lobbying hard for me, he was compelled to reconsider.

He gave me one week to get to Leysin, Switzerland. I raced a World Cup event in Toronto, then flew directly from there to Switzerland. I was scared to death. Brett picked me up at the airport at 11 a.m.

(after waiting two hours for my delayed flight), and my suitcase didn't arrive—just my bike. I was intimidated by him, and during the entire drive, he read me the riot act, telling me I needed to let go of everything any other coach had ever taught me and pretend I'd just retired. He said we no longer had any expectations for winning any particular races or making any teams. This was all about me becoming the best I could be. Listen to him and do things his way, he said, and I would be guaranteed my best-ever results. I was embarking on a journey to find myself—triathlon was just the vehicle for self-discovery.

When we pulled into camp, Brett told me I'd be going straight into a turbo trainer session.

"But I don't have my suitcase with any of my clothes," I told him.

"Well, we have your bike and the clothes on your back," he said. "Those will have to do, and if not, maybe you can borrow something from Loretta."

I couldn't wait to see Loretta. I desperately needed to see a friendly face after such a long trip to a beautiful but wildly unfamiliar and, frankly, scary place. Brett showed me to the gym, where Loretta was hammering away on her bike trainer.

"Loretta, hey!" I waved.

She didn't even look at me.

What a bitch, I fumed. *She invited me here, and now she can't even be bothered to say hello?* I didn't get it.

Brett set me up on the trainer, and I rode for two hours in my jeans and T-shirt. Thankfully, Loretta dropped the ice-queen act as we pedaled side by side and caught up. I think she had just been playing it cool in front of Brett.

The next morning, I woke up nervous but eager to join the squad for swim practice. The pool was about 12 miles straight downhill from camp. I learned that we'd be riding our bikes to the pool, which sounded like a nice warm-up. When we arrived, Brett outlined the 6-km set. I was accustomed to swimming 3-km workouts—that was a big swim day—and by the end of the workout, I thought my arms might fall off. I narrowly survived.

I also survived my introduction to the squad's military-style ethos. When I said "Good job" to a woman in my lane after we gutted out a tough set, Brett made it clear that my "cheerleading" was not only discouraged—it was not tolerated. Brett didn't want me disrupting the stringent atmosphere he'd deliberately established. You put your head down and went to work. There would be no muddling around blowing sunshine up anyone's backside. Deep down, that brutally honest approach resonated with me. I thought back to when I was 12 and my dad had let me win a tennis match and how irate it had made me. I'd always believed he was sincere in his praise—he told me all the time that I was a great athlete—and when I realized he was disingenuously letting me win, it made me question every piece of praise he'd ever uttered. I've never wanted to be fooled into thinking I was good at something if I wasn't. Tell it like it is, so I can improve. I knew Brett would give it to me straight and that his observations would only make me better.

Now that the biggest workout of the day was out of the way, my thoughts turned to breakfast and a nap. But first I had to find Brett's van to hitch a ride back up to camp. Oddly, it was not where it had been parked.

"Get dressed; we ride home," said Loretta, seeing that I was clearly not with the program.

My heart sank.

"Are you kidding me?" I whined. "I'm starving, Loretta!"

"Just go with Jane; she's slow. You'll be fine," she answered before disappearing up the hill.

Jane dropped me in the first five minutes. If she was the weak link, what did that make me?

I slogged up that merciless mountain for an hour and a half and fell into a hot bath when I got back to my room. I was inhaling my breakfast when I heard a pounding on my door followed by an announcement that we'd be leaving in a half hour and that I should meet the others at the van, ready to run. A shakeout jog would probably do me good after that grind up the hill, I thought. I changed into my run gear, filled my water bottle, and made my way to the squad van. Waiting for the others, I figured I'd use the bathroom one last time, so I set my water bottle on the roof of the van and ran back to my room. When I returned a few minutes later, I noticed that there was just an ounce of water remaining in my bottle. *What the hell?*

"Does anyone know what happened to my water?" I asked.

"You should've drunk enough after your last session and come prepared," Brett hissed.

I ducked into the van and stared blankly out the window as we coasted down the hill again. When we got to the bottom, Brett pulled over and let us out. He said he'd meet us back at camp and then pulled off the dirt shoulder, leaving a cloud of dust to settle over us.

I looked around, desperate for any gesture of commiseration—an understanding smile, a knowing wince—but received none.

Two hours and 15 minutes later, I stumbled into my room, absolutely destroyed. I called my mom in tears.

"I'm not going to survive this," I cried.

But every day, Brett would give me an impossible task, and somehow I would manage to get it done. I couldn't move my arms over my head, yet I'd get in the pool and manage to crank out 6 km. And every night, I'd call my mom and tell her I couldn't possibly endure another day.

Of course I left the weepy calls to M out of my dispatch for USA Triathlon:

> It is now Day 7 at Brett's training camp. . . . I'm so proud of myself for having been strong enough to come here and survive this first week and for having the determination. I'm starting to feel I'm capable of so much more than I ever thought. This, to me, is an amazing feeling. Brett has a way of drawing you in and making you feel that priority number one should be achieving my goals: podium in a World Cup and having the best preparation for whatever I face. His belief, and I must agree, is to do everything right so that I haven't left any stone unturned. It makes perfect sense, but I can't help to feel a deep sadness in my heart for missing home, my family, pets and friends. The other half of my heart seems to feel like I'm doing the right thing. Satisfying that yearning to be the very best that I can be. I will take one day at a time after Sydney, depending on what happens, I will reassess.

I had reached a point with my swimming where I thought I physically couldn't go any harder. Brett told me my stroke was far from perfect—I had a weak finish/exit phase and breathed only to my right. But instead of trying to fully retrain my stroke to make it technically perfect, he took what felt natural to me and focused on creating efficiency and strength. He invented all sorts of training tools—drag suits, bands, and strangely shaped paddles that came down to my elbows. He designed paddles to keep me from bending at the wrist, and there was a serrated edge that would dig into my wrist if I bent it too much. I would wear them for a long set and get out of the pool with blood running down my forearms. They left scars that made it look like I'd attempted suicide, and I didn't pay much attention to them until I started getting concerned looks from strangers at the grocery store. But the paddles worked. Brett kept right on experimenting with my stroke even if it was two weeks before a race.

Brett gave me impossibly hard sets that brought me to the edge of my limits and then pushed me past them. He'd yell at me to go faster, and I'd tell him I was going as fast as I could. He forcefully disagreed.

I had no idea how many more levels of pain I could experience. Brett introduced to me what real hurt was.

"You need to face the pain and not be afraid of it," he'd tell me.

The bike and run workouts were equally excruciating. In some sessions, there were moments when I wasn't sure if I would be alive or dead the next minute. *Is my heart going to jump out of my chest? Am I going to be sick?* Pure, unadulterated pain pulsed through every cell in my body.

But on the other side, I was rewarded with the most incredible feeling of accomplishment. It was euphoria. Bliss.

I was already intimately familiar with the idea that you have to be comfortable being uncomfortable. But this was the next level. I didn't know if I could sustain the intensity of each effort—and honestly, it didn't really matter. I learned to race that way.

On race mornings, I would have my breakfast and go back through my training journal to review all the work I'd done to reassure myself that I was poised to have a great performance. Then I'd break down in tears on the hotel-room floor because I knew it was going to be a physically agonizing experience. *How much pain can I withstand?* The anticipation led me to a total meltdown before every race.

From day one, Brett made no secret of his opinion that one of the biggest things holding me back was my weight. At that very first swim session, I walked out on the pool deck, and Brett had me step onto a scale in front of my new squadmates—athletes I'd idolized for years.

"Whoa, you've got to lose some weight!" he pronounced. I was 5 feet 9 inches and 139 pounds.

"You guys better wait until after Siri gets in the pool, because there's going to be a tidal wave when she jumps in, and you might drown," he cracked.

Naturally, I was mortified, but I did my best to let it roll off my (apparently ample) backside. Stealing a quick glance at Loretta, I could see the concern on her face. I think everyone in earshot was cringing inside a little.

Before I went to Brett, I'd had a generally positive body image. I didn't feel self-conscious walking around in my bathing suit at the beach or at a race. I was comfortable in my skin and accepted my big, muscular butt (which Brett likened to "rabbits in a sack") and thighs from years of playing hockey and lacrosse. Maybe I was a little softer than some of my competitors, but I was strong and healthy. (Once at a World Cup race in Paris, someone told me, "You run pretty fast for a big girl!" but I blew it off after my Boulder training partner Pat reassured me that the comment was absurd.) But Brett was right that dropping some weight would increase my chances of winning races. He told me that losing roughly 8 pounds would shave a minute and a half off my 10K run time without any other change to my training.

Brett knew I would do anything to win races, and if losing weight was part of the equation, I was all in. He prescribed a plan of attack.

"At camp we have the cheesecake squad, and we have the lettuce squad," Brett explained. "You're definitely on the lettuce squad. All I want you to eat is lettuce, tomatoes, vegetables—that's it."

I asked him how I was going to have any energy, and he explained that there are carbohydrates in vegetables.

Even before the weight discussion came up, I would get in the bath every night and thank my body for working so hard to let me perform. I knew enough about nutrition to understand that I had to give my body the fuel it needed to do what I was asking of it day after day. Adopting the diet of a rabbit wasn't the answer.

I cut out the starchy carbs except for my morning peanut butter on toast. I ate huge salads and a lot of rotisserie chicken. Dinner was often a piece of fish and a side of vegetables. I was hungry a lot of the time but felt like I was still honoring my body and protecting my health. I started losing the weight, landing at a new racing weight of 130 pounds, and a few weeks later at the pool, Brett gushed about how amazing I looked. "You look like a thoroughbred," he said. Sure enough, my run times began to drop. Coach was smug with satisfaction.

Brett was a masterful architect when it came to designing training programs that produced the maximum benefit from each session. He considered each athlete separately and determined what each person could handle and what type of training delivered the best results. Sometimes there'd be 10 of us in the pool, and everyone would be doing a different workout.

Each day I would do a key workout with complementary sessions that promoted active recovery or helped tune the aerobic engine. If I did a hard 5-km swim in the morning followed by 10 1-km treadmill repeats, Brett would have me get out on the bike for an easy 2-hour ride to spin out the lactate in my legs. When he said to go hard, I went all out, and when he said to go easy, I went easy. If someone in the group was going too hard on a prescribed easy ride and started to get away from me, I would turn into a raging bitch on wheels. Trying to follow Coach's directions to a T and do the right thing—keep it easy—while being made to feel slow and weak when someone surged and dropped me was frustrating beyond belief, and I made no secret of it.

We'd put together 10 days of hard training, and then on the 11th day, we'd get a break, maybe just an easy swim. Luckily, I learned that I could bounce back with just a day's recovery. I also learned that even if I felt absolutely exhausted, I could still rally.

Brett keyed in to precisely what had been holding me back. I didn't *believe* I had the toughness or strength to truly be great. He knew I had to prove to myself that I could achieve the seemingly impossible. So every day, he dished out an inconceivable (in my mind) goal, and every day I tackled it, always surprised by my own grit and guts.

My first World Cup race under Brett was in August 2000 in Hungary. I arrived at the start line so sore and dog tired from my training that I didn't know how I was going to finish, let alone race well. But when the start gun fired, my mind clicked into race mode, and I felt strong and in control of my performance. To my amazement and absolute joy, I ended up finishing second, after Loretta. All the hard training had paid dividends. I was happy that Loretta had won—it was an incredible comeback after a year and a half spent recovering from a broken leg and dealing with legal battles over the Australian Olympic team selection (she ultimately made the team).

Six days later, I had another World Cup event, this time in the medieval city of Lausanne, Switzerland. M had attended the university there, and we were happy to be able to spend some time together in this ultracharming European city. The night before the race, we went out for dinner and ended up eating full meals at two different restaurants because I was so hungry.

I arrived on the Lausanne start line exhausted but tried to remain optimistic. Two-time ITU world champ Michellie Jones of Australia was the one to beat—she was winning everything. Brett instructed me to shadow her in the race. I was to stay on her feet in the swim, sit on her wheel on the bike, and run on her heels. I stuck to the plan, and a couple of kilometers into the run, the pace started to feel easy, so I surged into the lead. As I started to pull away from Michellie, I felt a pang of fear that this was too good to be true. Even though I was opening up a lead, I still heard her breath like she was right on my shoulder. I wouldn't let up, even if I could afford to. I held my pace and place to break my first finish-line tape at a World Cup race.

I couldn't believe it—the moment was both surreal and deeply satisfying. I had proven to myself that I deserved to be racing among the world's best. I belonged. Runner-up Brigitte McMahon crossed the finish line 36 seconds later, and Michellie placed third, more than a minute after I'd finished.

After the race, I received a handwritten note from Brett. It was easier for him to express praise and emotion in letters. He wrote, "I am just proud that I was able to help you fulfill one of your long-held goals. . . . Sunday you fulfilled your potential of that day. . . . I am so pleased you took the opportunity by the throat and made it yours; may we have many more, but that's your decision. I only promise I will always do my best." Making Brett proud felt unbelievably gratifying—he'd taken a huge leap of faith in me, and I had delivered. *We'd* done it.

I went to Wollongong, Australia, for a Team USA training camp, and I felt like an outcast the entire time. I don't think the other American athletes or our governing body, USAT, liked that I was being funded at home but training and racing with some success out of the country. USAT wanted all the best American athletes to come out of its development program in Colorado Springs, not from the controversial Brett Sutton in Switzerland. I tried hard to get the USAT people to like me—I went out of my way to be polite and gracious, but I always got the cold shoulder and felt like they secretly didn't want me to succeed. One morning, while flipping through the newspaper over breakfast, I spotted a picture of the team at a welcome dinner the previous evening and I was hurt that I hadn't been invited. I had been feeling so down about the whole Olympics situation that I invited my mom to come with me so we could make a short vacation of the trip. We stayed in a different hotel than the team and did everything by ourselves.

I was still training hard in Wollongong because there was a glimmer of hope that I might get to race. Jennifer Gutierrez was nursing a running injury, and since I'd just won the Lausanne race against the best women in the world, I thought I might be selected to start in her place.

One afternoon I went to the track to run 25 × 400s, leaving on 2 minutes. Venezuelan pro triathlete Gilberto González happened to be there (he had made the Olympic team) and ended up doing half of the session with me. A photographer was there, and a picture of me appeared in the next day's local newspaper, which I heard annoyed the "real" Team USA. I finished the workout really excited that I'd clocked a 1:13 average. And then, still catching my breath, I fell to the ground in tears. *Who cares? What's the point of all of this, anyway?* I was just going to be watching from the sidelines. It seemed like a cruel waste.

Despite being treated like an outsider, I was discouraged by USAT from leaving camp for a few days to train with Loretta, who was in Sydney preparing for her first Games. I desperately needed to be around my good friend and training partner, so I left anyway. It was Loretta—not my own team or federation—who ended up securing seats for my mom and me to watch the Olympic race.

Attending the Olympics as an alternate was an emotional roller coaster. I did my best to mask my disappointment. I cheered loudly for my friends but wished with all my heart that I could be in the mix with them. When I saw Brigitte (gold), Michellie (silver), and Magali Messmer (bronze)—all of whom I'd beaten in Lausanne—on the Olympic dais accepting their medals, I couldn't help but imagine myself up there with them.

After reading a race report written by some of the US Olympic team members, Brett wrote USA Triathlon a scathing letter for overlooking me when I had the track record to prove that I was entitled to be there. In his view, the American debut in the Olympic triathlon had been a complete flop.

"Personally, as a coach, I would have been apologizing to the nation, and with the talent base the US has, contemplating resignation for a failed campaign," he wrote. He reminded them that I'd beaten the Olympic podium finishers handily in Lausanne and pointed out that there had plenty of time to add me to the team roster. "It was a total failure on every level, and that should not be excused by the euphoria of a first-time Olympics," he concluded.

After all was said and done, I found myself in an emotional tailspin, and I just wanted to go home to Colorado. I told Brett that I was over it. He said, no, I wouldn't be going home—I'd be coming to Switzerland for two weeks to train for the duathlon world championship in France. If I didn't, I'd have to find a new coach.

Two days later, I flew to Switzerland. It was just Brett, Aussies Matt Reed and Jane Fardell, and me. We trained harder than ever.

I went off to Du world's with zero expectations. I'd never raced a duathlon before, let alone at a world championship, so it was a big experiment. It was one of the hardest physical challenges of my life, but I surprised myself by finishing second. I barely lost gold to Steph Forrester in a photo finish. I couldn't walk for a week after the race, but it lifted me out of my post-Sydney funk.

"See, there are so many things you can do—the Olympics is just one day," Brett told me. He was right—I was back on the horse.

The steady, shining light throughout all of my highs and lows was M's presence at my races. Words can't express how much it meant to me—to us both—to share those experiences. I could always be myself around M, and she graciously put up with whatever I dished out. I'd be intense and nervous before a race, and she'd take care of my every need and even massage my feet. We'd get to our hotel room, and she'd venture out and buy the peanut butter and bananas, get a fan if it was hot, take my bike to the shop—whatever I needed. After the race, I'd apologize profusely for being so difficult and make sure she knew how much I appreciated her. She wore the same red baseball cap to every race (for good luck and also so I could spot her in the crowd) and cheered not just for me but for the other racers as well. Everyone got to know and love her. She was the ultimate sidekick.

Brett told me many times, "Your biggest weakness is love. Love makes you soft." He didn't want M at any of my training camps or races. He said our relationship was codependent and that it made me weak. (He was also wary of my relationship with Loretta.)

Not for a second did I consider compromising my tight-knit relationship with M. She was as instrumental to realizing my triathlon dreams as I was, and having her along for this journey had brought us close again. But I didn't tell Brett that. She'd still come to my camps and races and keep a low profile. After winning a race, I'd talk to Brett on the phone, and he'd say, "I told you you'd get stronger if you let go of that relationship."

"Yeah, you're right, Coach," I'd reply, my mom sitting there right next to me.

Loretta also supported me on many levels. She was much more than my training partner—she helped me grow as a person. When I first joined the squad, I would always get my own room at races. She'd ask me if I wanted to room together to save money, and I'd decline, saying something like "I like to get up early and drink my coffee and not feel like I'm in anybody's way." She'd shrug it off, deeply annoyed, I'm sure. But back at camp, it made sense for us to become roommates, so we did.

I'd go to the grocery store and get just enough food to make myself dinner, and she'd walk in and say, "Really? You didn't think to ask if I wanted dinner, too?" She made me think about considering the needs of another person when I was accustomed to thinking only of myself. "You'll never be in a relationship if you act like that," she said. It was an important wake-up call.

When I came out to Loretta, I was worried she'd reject me.

"I don't want to make you uncomfortable and hope it doesn't change the way you feel about me, but I need you to know I'm gay," I told her.

"I know you're gay, Siri, and I don't care," she said. "But seriously, it's pretty shitty that you're just talking to me about this now—I'm supposed to be your best friend."

Loretta and I were inseparable, and I worried that people would think we were more than friends if they ever found out I was gay. When I expressed my concern to Loretta, she said she couldn't care less what people thought. "They'll just have to get a grip," she replied. I couldn't have been more relieved or grateful for the sincerity of her friendship.

Now that everything was out in the open, I felt unconditional acceptance and a deepened connection. I was relieved that my sexual preference was truly a nonissue.

Leading up to a race, Loretta would again serve as my shrink. "Siri, you're really good; there's no need to get worked up like this," she'd insist. "Go into this race knowing that you're the best. If you don't win this, I'm going to kick your ass because you should win." But in my mind, she was the real star. Loretta's well-rounded, exceptional athletic talent and toughness were deeply inspiring and motivating, and toeing the line in the same race always scared the shit out of me but also coaxed out my best effort. I knew if I could start the run less than 3 minutes back from her, I could have a shot at winning; any more than 3 minutes, and she'd be impossible to beat.

Loretta indulged my competitive nature in training, too. During one training camp in Australia, we took off for a 1.5-hour run and were supposed to run the last 40 minutes as hard as we could. We were about a kilometer from finishing, and I was fading. I was a stronger runner—Loretta, a front-pack swimmer, always led from the start of a race, whereas I came from behind—but she was hot-stepping me. I actually started grabbing at her shirt. "Piss off!" she said, batting my hands away. I literally tackled her to the ground to keep her from dropping me.

There was a time when Loretta and I were ranked number one and number two in the world and were each other's biggest rivals. But we honestly didn't care who finished first or second as long as it was one of us.

In late 2000, Brett wanted to move the camp from Leysin to Valle du Joux, and a lot of the athletes didn't want to go. They said we had to rally together and tell Brett we weren't going anywhere. I wasn't willing to do that—I was getting results with his help and would follow him anywhere. I became alienated from a lot of my squadmates because they lost bargaining power without me getting on board. Loretta wanted to stay and support the other athletes but told me to do whatever I needed to do.

Around that time, an Englishwoman named Annie Emmerson joined the squad, and she, Loretta, and I soon became inseparable. I'd also met Annie on a bus ride when we were at a race in the Czech Republic and had seen her at a few races after that. Annie, a tremendously talented runner, maintained a healthy sense of humor despite the pressures of training. We'd turn up at a morning swim workout knowing we had a hard 7 km on the schedule and give each other a sympathetic look and chuckle. We were triathlon's version of Charlie's Angels, with Brett as our Bosley. Annie and Loretta provided a daily spark of inspiration and pushed me to draw the very best out of myself, both in and out of training.

We started a weekly pizza-and-wine-night tradition where we could stray from our super-strict diets. I looked forward to these nights like a kid anticipating Christmas morning—they went a long way in relieving the stresses of camp. After stuffing myself on pizza and building a nice wine buzz, I'd go home and crank out my prebedtime ritual of 200 abdominal crunches on the floor of our tiny living room while the BBC news blared from the TV. I never missed my nightly crunches. Loretta thought it was silly and annoying, but of course she had to join in.

Ten days before the 2001 world championship in Edmonton, Alberta, Loretta, Annie, and I decided to reward ourselves after a long training day with a margarita from the lobby bar in our building. One margarita turned into four. The next morning at swim practice, I was nursing a bad hangover. Brett asked what was wrong.

"I think we just ate something last night that disagreed with us," said Loretta. We didn't dare mention the dozen margaritas we'd consumed among us.

After the swim, Brett said he wanted the three of us to do an easy jog. We laced up, and a few minutes out on the trail, I tripped over a root and flew 10 feet into the air. Loretta and Annie laughed so hard they wet their pants. They were the best friends I could've asked for.

My main goal for the 2000 and 2001 seasons had been to get my swimming good enough to have me coming out with the lead pack in World Cup races. I knew if I could do this, my odds of winning races would go way up. Because Loretta was a phenomenal swimmer, she was my marker in swim training.

At a World Cup race in France, I tore my plantar fascia when I stepped on a rock during the swim exit. (I seemed to somehow tear this muscle every year, which would take me out of run training for a month each time.) I was in great pain but still managed to eke out the win. I couldn't run for two weeks after that race, and I had the qualifying race for the 2001 ITU world championship in just three weeks in Shreveport, Louisiana. I had no choice if I wanted to make it to the Edmonton world's start line—I had to race in Shreveport. I flew from Switzerland to the race, which was a total disaster. I couldn't kick in the swim, so I immediately lost the pack. I rode the entire 40K alone, then took three steps into the run and immediately fell over. I couldn't support the weight of my body on my bad foot. I was sure my world championship dream was dead.

I decided to go to Canada with my training group. I could train with them as they prepped for Edmonton, and I'd jump into a World Cup race in Toronto that was to be held two weeks before the Edmonton world championship. I tried to focus on having a solid performance in Toronto.

It was a breakthrough race. For the first time, I came out of the water with the lead women. The race could've ended after the swim, and I still would have been happy. I'd worked so hard on my swim, and now I'd matched the ability of the "swimmers" of our sport. I felt even better when I crossed the finish line in first place.

After the race, the mother of another pro woman in the race approached Loretta and said, "Siri Lindley is clearly on something to race like that." This woman had no idea that Loretta and I were best friends. Loretta gave it to her straight.

"Excuse me, Siri is my training partner, and I can guarantee you that she works her ass off and rightfully earned that win." Then she turned and walked away.

Brett said that he wanted me to race the ITU Aquathlon World Championships, held the Wednesday before the Triathlon World Championships, just in case I wasn't given a start on Sunday. He wanted me to have a shot at a world champion crown. I raced and won, beating Olympian Sheila Taormina. I was on cloud nine.

As in nearly every ITU world championship I'd attended since 1996, I didn't find out that I'd been accepted to compete until the day before the race. Libby Burrell, the high-performance and national team program director for USAT (her job was to pick athletes for certain races and establish selection guidelines), had been fighting to keep me off the Edmonton start list because I hadn't fulfilled the qualifying criteria by finishing in Shreveport. I went to the ITU and made my case. I told them how desperately I wanted to race, that I had just won in Toronto and was ranked number two in the world. They didn't hesitate to let me in, as they wanted all of the best athletes in the world on the Edmonton start line. I was relieved and grateful to the ITU for the chance to race, but it was hard to see my own country trying to get in the way of my opportunity to race.

Loretta told me, "I'm putting my money on you for Edmonton." But I didn't want to hear that—I didn't need the added pressure. Winning a world championship seemed even more unattainable than an Olympic medal. At the Olympics, countries send their best three athletes, but at the world championship, the field goes even deeper.

I had a bad start and a horrible swim. I came out of the water at the very back of the third pack, and part of me wanted to give up right there, but I heard Brett's voice in my head telling me to let it go, push on to the best of my ability, and seize any opportunities.

Onto the bike, I was on a mission to get as close to the front as possible. I drove hard to catch the second pack and then reached the front of the group. I put my head down and hammered to reach the front pack. A Belgian racer named Kathleen Smet was one of a few women who helped me catch the front pack. With about 2 kilometers to go, Michellie Jones, who had been conserving energy so she could unleash her dangerous run, rode up beside me.

"That was silly doing all the work—you need to learn to be smarter," she said. "Now you've trashed yourself." She was trying to get in my head going into the run.

I kept on the throttle.

"Hey, Michellie, you ready to run?" I said as I started to pull away.

Due to the late decision to let me race, my transition spot was at the very back of the transition area, meaning I had a longer distance to run after parking my bike. I was lit from within like never before and sprinted out of transition. By the end of the 400-meter blue carpet that led out onto the run course, I had taken the lead with a trail of about 30 women on my heels. Even after dropping Michellie, I ran the entire 10K absolutely flat out. I was running for my life and was further spurred on by Brett, dressed in a full suit and screaming at the top of his lungs, "You haven't won anything yet! Go! Go! Go!"

I didn't take my foot off the gas until I broke the tape—this time as world champion.

TOP

Lisa and I (and our dog Lulu) had some of our happiest times in Point O' Woods, Fire Island.

BOTTOM

Growing up, I thought my mom was the most beautiful woman in the world. Black-tie dinners were a regular affair when she was married to Frank Gifford.

TOP

George Steinbrenner would give us his box seats for the Kansas City Royals games. George Brett was a family friend—funny and engaging.

BOTTOM LEFT

I had a good showing in my first 5K—wearing my favorite polo shirt.

BOTTOM RIGHT

Uncle Boyce was an Olympic gold medalist in eight-man crew in 1964. He always told me I could be a great athlete.

ABOVE

Coach Renee Spellman was my greatest mentor. She also introduced me to lacrosse, and I went on to be the team captain at Brown.

LEFT

For my triathlon debut in Englewood, Colorado, I rented a very heavy 10-speed. I thought it was rad.

7
PowerBar
Carnac

OPPOSITE

In the early days I was excited to be doing something I was passionate about. Speedo and PowerBar were my first sponsors.

ABOVE

My pre-race prayer ritual took the edge off as I waited to be called to the start at the 1999 world championships in Montreal.

LEFT

My first time racing Mrs. T's Chicago Triathlon, an iconic event that drew all the top pros.

TOP

If it wasn't for Lynn Oski, I wouldn't have discovered triathlon. She was my idol, best friend, and first real teacher in the sport.

BELOW

Once I moved to Boulder and turned pro, I met Pat Brown. We became fast friends and regular training partners, balancing the hard work with laughter.

OPPOSITE

I fell in love with running thanks to Whoopi, a faithful friend who brought me endless joy. She even ran with me at the track!

BRASI
RLX
17
30
USA
SPEEDO

LEFT

Just two weeks after choking at the Olympic Trials in Sydney, I raced the world championships in Perth. Loretta Harrop and Joanne King were signing autographs, and I asked for Loretta's autograph even though I would be racing against her the next day!

OPPOSITE, BOTTOM

Mom and me at the 2000 World Cup in Cancún, Mexico. I was first out of the water after dolphin diving the last 200 meters and went on to win the race.

BELOW

I qualified to be an alternate for the 2000 US Olympic triathlon team at the trials in Dallas. I joined Brett Sutton's squad later that summer.

TOP

My win at the ITU Aquathlon World Championship four days prior to the start of the 2001 world championships in Edmonton lifted my confidence. I exited the swim with the lead women for the first time.

BOTTOM

At the 2001 world's, my bike rack was at the far end of the transition area, but I wouldn't be deterred. I exited T2 in the lead.

OPPOSITE

Winning the world championship in 2001 was the most amazing feeling. I was incredibly blessed to find what I needed to make my dream come true.

CHAMPIONSHIP
EDMONTON 2001 ITU
TRIATHLON WORLD
CHAMPIONSHIP
TRIATHLON WORLD
CHAMPIONSHIP
USA
SPEEDO
EDMONTON 2001
60
FILA

101

OPPOSITE

At the 2002 ITU World Cup in Lausanne, I came off the bike to find a big fence blocking the run course, so I climbed over it. I lost my 10-second gap when they opened the gate, but the adrenaline helped me recover quickly and win.

TOP LEFT

Brett Sutton rarely went to races, but Loretta Harrop and I paid for his trip to the 2001 world championships. I am forever grateful to both of them.

E

my dad and mom after my world pionship win in 2001, one of the mes the three of us had been together out 20 years.

T

002 ITU World Championship in Cancún not my race to win, but I finished the on as the winner of the World Cup series second consecutive year. I retired soon after.

RIGHT

In 2012 Leanda Cave won in Kona following her 70.3 world championship a month before. We made an amazing team.

MIDDLE

I loved my broadcasting work with NBC, which included the Hy-Vee Triathlon (here with pro Laura Bennett) and the Life Time Fitness Triathlon broadcasts with Ted Robinson.

BOTTOM

Team Sirius 2013: Damon Barnett, Mirinda Carfrae, Mauro Cavanha, Leanda Cave, Jenny Fletcher, Dede Griesbauer, Rebekah Keat, Carol Menezes, Raphael Menezes, Kathy Rakel, Jonathan Shearon, Amanda Stevens, and me.

ABOVE

Mirinda and I after her third Ironman world championship win in 2014. My passion for triathlon remains as strong as ever because of people like Rinny.

LEFT

The trust, respect, and communication that I establish with my athletes are hard-won, but they deliver success.

TOP

My dogs always bring a smile to my face. Since I was a little girl, animals have made me feel loved and safe.

BOTTOM

My wife, Bek, is the love of my life and my constant inspiration. Words cannot describe the flood of emotion I experienced on our wedding day.

7

CHAMPION

I CAN'T BELIEVE IT. *I did it. Me.*

Winning the 2001 world championships was an out-of-body experience. I had achieved an impossible dream and couldn't wrap my head around the magnitude of the moment. Amid the sense of suspended reality, the overwhelming feeling was gratitude. I felt an immense appreciation for every single blessing in my life, past and present. I stood atop that podium as the person I'd always yearned to be—strong, resilient, undaunted.

Winning the world title validated this truth: If you want something badly enough—if the desire dwells deep in your bones, and you are committed to facing any obstacle with tenacity and courage—you will prevail. I am living proof of this beautiful, abiding truth.

Still in a starry daze, I was gathering myself in the finish-line area when the mother of another top competitor walked up to me. I'd noticed that M had gone over to congratulate this woman's daughter on her race, and I thought it was a kind gesture for this mom to return the favor. But when I looked into her face, her expression betrayed a different agenda.

"They're not doing drug testing?" she asked, her tone accusatory. "So you're not getting tested? What's *wrong* with these people?"

I was gutted. I had just experienced the greatest moment of my athletic life, and this spiteful woman was questioning the legitimacy of it with her cruel barb. The insinuation devastated me, and then it pissed me off. In truth, the US Anti-Doping Agency tested for performance-enhancing drugs at every ITU race I'd ever done, and I was also tested randomly outside competition.

"You want to test my blood?" I replied, sticking out my arm. "I'll give you my blood right now. Take it all, and go do your test."

She abruptly turned around and walked away, still shaking her head as she disappeared into the finish-line crowd. I did my best to let it go and refocus on the people who were there to share this moment with me—my mom, my dad, Brett, Annie, and Loretta. When Libby Burrell came up to congratulate me, I was gracious but thought, *Really?*

Loretta could have won that day (she finished eighth), and I didn't know how to act around her. Was it okay to be excited that I had won? I wanted to savor the victory, but I was also sensitive to her disappointment about her own race. But Loretta celebrated my win as if it were her own. She made congratulatory signs and posted them all around the door of my hotel room and rallied us to go celebrate.

"Tomorrow I can be bummed about my race, but today we celebrate yours," she said. Loretta's completely selfless and supportive reaction made that milestone day even more meaningful. The icing on the cake was when she dug up my Lenny Kravitz CD and had the race officials introduce me at the awards ceremony to the song "American Woman."

My dad was front and center at the banquet. He had a big, round belly, and one of his favorite jokes was saying it was clear where I'd gotten my athletic physique. It was classic Dad: He'd charm all my friends with his quick wit and easy sense of humor. But it wasn't the complete picture. Ever since he'd remarried and started a new family, he'd been completely checked out from my life. He had come to a few major races, but M had been there for all of them. She'd cried with me in my lowest moments and celebrated my highest. With both M and my dad sitting in the audience at the awards banquet, I felt like I had to thank them equally. My mom had been the only one I'd been able to lean on day in, day out, yet in my speech I gave my dad the same acknowledgment. It didn't feel fair or sit right with me—I just didn't want to disappoint him or hurt his feelings. I wish that instead of trying to please and protect him, I'd spoken the words my heart knew to be true.

A couple of weeks after Edmonton, I was still riding high on my world title win when I received an e-mail from Brett.

> Dear Siri,
>
> No, dear champ,
>
> I give you credit for staging one of the greatest performances in triathlon short history. . . . It was 55 seconds to second and another 20 or 30 sec to third. Absolutely epic and you did that. Not me, not USAT, not anybody. S. Lindley from Colorado. 100%.

> My input helps you tap 85% of your talent till present and that's 25% more than your past. The good news, well good for you frightening for others, is that Coach Sutto truly believes you have 15% more improvement, 30 seconds at the run at least, not to mention the swim.
>
> So you don't say I don't give you credit, however, you must understand that my success rate is unmatched in any sport because I know how you think and how you react. The walking talking Siri does not fool me and you should be so glad it doesn't because it enables me to access your talent where others can't.

The letter went on to outline potential training and racing plans before he signed off with his trademark "Cheers, Sutto."

Brett, of all people, calling my Edmonton race "one of the greatest performances in triathlon" felt beyond amazing. There was no better praise.

Leveraging that momentum, I continued my season with World Cup wins in Newfoundland, Hungary, and Lausanne. It was an unreal ride—I won six big races in a row. I felt on top of the world. I was so appreciative of the ITU's support in Edmonton that when its president Les McDonald asked me on a few occasions to slow down in races—I was winning some races by 4 minutes—to let more women finish within points reach, I would walk the final 400 meters to the finish line, high-fiving cheering spectators. When Brett found out, he was livid. "Don't you fucking ever do that again," he told me. I was giving my competitors false confidence that they were getting closer to me, and I was setting them up to one day beat me. He was right, but I was desperate to have an ally in the ITU since USAT clearly didn't have my back.

After I won in Hungary, where Loretta finished 10th, again she was genuinely happy for me. We partied late into the night—the small town of Tiszaújváros staged the best post-race festivities on the race circuit, with music, dancing, and drinking in the streets—and got back to the hotel a couple of hours before our scheduled 3 a.m. airport shuttle. M, who'd been asleep for hours when I finally got back to our room, had to pack up my bike because the room was spinning. She had absolutely no idea what she was doing. When I finally started to regain my wits in the shuttle van, I looked over at my bike bag in the bench seat behind me. There was a wheel peeking out at one end and my seat post jutting out at the other. It was an absolute jumble of a mess, and we laughed until I couldn't tell if my stomach hurt more from the alcohol or M's hack packing job. I couldn't have loved her more. That night remains one of my favorite memories from my years racing abroad.

Despite my success, I felt a nagging sense that something bad was going to happen to counter my good fortune. Back at camp in Switzerland, I told Loretta, "I'm scared because I can't believe how happy I am right now. I've never felt so content and at peace." It was too good to be true. I couldn't shake the expectation that something awful was going to send me hurtling back to earth. When you're used to feeling angst all the time, happiness seems unnatural and uneasy.

My state of mind was a pendulum swing from being deeply content to being absolutely phobic about what misery surely awaited. But being at camp in Switzerland—doing what I loved most in an enchanting mountain enclave frozen in time—connected me to my faith. Every time I had to walk the mile to the phone booth, I marveled at how absolutely stunning my surroundings were and felt immense gratitude for the opportunity to be there. I was acutely aware of my blessings, of the gifts and grace of God. I've always considered myself more spiritual than religious, and I drew motivation for racing from my desire to express my boundless gratitude for my many blessings. The best way to appreciate my gifts and ability was to utilize them to the fullest extent. That meant giving my absolute everything—heart and soul—when the start gun fired. Racing well was a means of honoring and appreciating my God-given ability and work ethic. I found confidence in my strengthening connection to faith. Rather than hope, I *knew* everything would be okay. Sure, I had overcome challenges in the past, but it hadn't always been pretty. Now I was getting through life in a way I was proud of—with hard work, trust, hope, and gratitude. Living in my body felt safer than it ever had.

In addition to my revitalized faith, Brett played an essential role in my mental shift. He helped me let go of some of the self-defeating tendencies that were holding me back. He taught me that I needed to get out of my own way to be the best athlete—and person—I could be.

"Your biggest challenge is for you to conquer yourself," he'd tell me. "Once you learn to control your thoughts, the contest with your opponent becomes easy. You need to have one focus: doing the very best that you can at every moment. Focusing on winning or losing the external contest will only lead to performance paralysis."

After the Olympics debacle, I'd wanted to win too much for my own good. Brett helped rewire my brain to sidestep what he called my "winning obsession."

In pre-race interviews, I'd always get asked which athletes I had an extra-close eye on going into the race. Without fail, I'd respond, "I'm only worried about myself because I'm the only one that I can control. All I can do is focus on myself and do my best every step of the way. The minute I start focusing on other athletes around me is the minute I start taking the energy away from myself." That answer served as an ongoing self-reminder. It became my mantra.

Certainly, I was no stranger to the pressures of race day, but maintaining my drive and focus in training became an even greater preoccupation. I missed my family, friends, and pets back in Boulder, but more than that, I began to crave a lifestyle that wasn't so self-centered. I loved living in Switzerland and Australia and traveling the world with my two best friends, Annie and Loretta, but I was truly tired of it being all about me. For years, one prevailing thought had guided my life: *What do I need to do to be the best that I can be?* I wanted to start turning my attention outward, to think more about the needs of other people for once. I was tired of feeling selfish.

Still, I couldn't tune out the voice in my head saying I still had something to prove.

If you walk away now, everyone will think you're a one-season wonder.

I was bound and determined to prove that my dream 2001 season wasn't a fluke. I was the real deal. I thought if I could put together one more season of consistent results—not necessarily win everything, just stay in the top three in the world rankings—then I could retire on top, with no regrets or doubts of my rightful legacy.

In January 2002, I went to the Gold Coast in Australia to train with Loretta. RLX had recently dropped its sponsorship of Tim DeBoom and me—I don't think the company had budgeted enough money to be able to fulfill its end of the deal after we'd both won world titles in 2001, so it found a clause in the contract that allowed it to dump us a year early. But RLX waited until December to cut us loose, which didn't give me enough time to line up sponsors for the 2002 season. That time period as a newly crowned world champ should have been my biggest moneymaking opportunity, but I had only a shoe sponsorship by New Balance Japan, which also sponsored Loretta. I was obligated by my new shoe contract to race the two World Cup races in Japan or I wouldn't get paid. Brett thought Australia would be the ideal place to prep for these races.

On the morning of January 12, Loretta and I were out for an hour-long build run along the waterfront of the Gold Coast, near Brisbane. We were deep into the workout, and the pace was getting tough. We were so focused on keeping it together that we didn't notice when a car pulled up right next to us. It was Gary Snowsill, the father of Emma Snowsill, another ITU athlete and the girlfriend of Loretta's younger brother, Luke (also a promising triathlete). He started honking the horn wildly and yelling inaudibly out the window. We stopped and looked at Gary, trying to understand what was going on.

“Get in!” he shouted. “Luke’s been hit by a car.”

We jumped into Gary’s car, and 10 meters down the road we saw Brett standing there. He had no idea what was going on and asked where the hell we were going. Gary zoomed off before we could explain.

Loretta was in a panic, telling Gary to run the red light whenever he stopped the car. When we arrived at the hospital, we found Luke, 23, lying unconscious in a hospital bed. There was no visible sign of trauma on his body—he looked like he was sleeping. I spent the night with Loretta and her family on the waiting-room floor awaiting updates on Luke’s condition and prognosis. After an agonizingly long night, the doctor came into Luke’s room and explained the extent of his traumatic brain injury. There was no brain activity, and the life-support machine was the only thing keeping him alive.

I sat with Loretta at her brother’s bedside, at an absolute loss for what to say or do. She held his hand, looking intently at him as if trying to imprint every detail of his beautiful face on a mind already wild with grief. She asked me to massage his feet, which I did. I was eager to make myself useful, to do anything I could to be there for Loretta and her family. I could not fathom the depths of their pain.

The Harrop family ultimately decided to remove Luke from life support, and for the remainder of the day, his family and closest friends took turns sitting at his bedside, saying their heartbreaking good-byes.

The woman who’d struck Luke as he rode his bike was a heroin addict who was high when she swerved into him while driving a stolen car. Despite her prior drug offenses, she ended up getting only five years of jail time with the possibility of parole after just three years. I still don't understand how the legal system failed so horrifically.

Luke was so respected and well liked that there was an outpouring of support from around the world. The Harrop home was filled from floor to ceiling with flowers and cards. The family set up a memorial fund (and later a race) to honor Luke's memory, and the race is still ongoing today. I attended city council meetings to talk about the need for safer ride routes in the area and was part of an effort to build a criterium track for cyclists at the Runaway Bay Center where we trained.

I struggled to find motivation to train. If I did muster the effort to go for a ride, I'd break down in tears and have to pull over. But there were also moments of deep appreciation for my health, my life. For Loretta and Emma, training became a therapy of sorts. They desperately needed an outlet for their suffocating grief.

When Loretta came back for her first pool session, Brett gave us a set of 3,000 meters straight. I was shocked—and pissed. The decent thing would've been to give us an interval workout that forced us to focus on the clock. Not staring at the floor of the pool lap after lap with nothing to occupy our thoughts but raw grief. Loretta made it about 1,000 meters before she got out. Emma had to stop halfway down the lane and tread water because of her sobbing. It was unbearable to see my friends suffering so intensely.

Eventually, we began to feel that we were honoring Luke by getting out there and doing what he also loved so much—what he would've wanted us to be doing. I was so scared of saying the wrong thing or not saying the right thing when Loretta needed to hear it that I often didn't say much at all. I trod lightly but steadfastly around my best friend.

Loretta and I did every single training ride—from hard interval sessions to 3-hour rides—at the Nerang Criterium Circuit, which had 1-km, 2-km, and 1-mile loops that were all hilly. Loretta didn't want to worry her family by riding her bike on the roads where Luke had been killed, and she was scared to anyhow. We rode countless circles around that track, but the monotony was a small price to pay if it meant bringing any ease to Loretta and her family. The track's undulating terrain—and the required mental stamina—only made us stronger.

Loretta went into the qualifying race for the Manchester Commonwealth Games after three weeks of minimal training. Still, she won the Australian trials for the Games team, surprising herself. She crossed the finish line, grabbed her dad, and broke down in tears. I know her brother was with her every stroke and step of the way. After that race, she dove back into her training, building herself back up in body and mind.

My first race of the year was the Devonport Oceania Cup in March, which I won, followed two weeks later by a World Cup race in Geelong, where I finished third. My next race wasn't until Ishigaki in mid-May.

A couple of weeks before I was supposed to leave for Japan I tore my plantar fascia muscle in training. I really needed the sponsor money and kept training through the super-painful injury, even though I was hobbling through my sessions. I had a cortisone shot in my foot and flew to Ishigaki with a doctor's medical exemption note. The day after I arrived in Japan, I went to the head of the Japan Triathlon Union with my note saying I had received a cortisone shot as a necessary medical treatment.

"You used a steroid drug?" asked the incredulous official.

"No! You're not understanding me!" I said. "My doctor injected cortisone into my torn foot muscle to relieve the swelling so that I can race."

Fortunately, the ITU's Les McDonald was able to explain the situation more clearly, telling him that athletes must get cortisone shots sometimes and that it's not considered an infraction—I was following medical advice and had done nothing improper or unethical.

I hadn't run in a week when I lined up on race day. My grandmother Lucille "Lucky" Lindley had passed away a few days earlier, and I badly wanted to have a strong race to honor her. I put the foot pain out of my mind and tried to think of the incredible woman who had offered a safe and happy refuge to me as a child. I felt guilty and sad about not being able to go to her funeral, but I could still pay tribute by doing my very best when that start gun sounded.

I swam and biked my absolute heart out. But my plantar fascia muscle had completely torn, and I hobbled to the finish in seventh place. I had to be carried back to my hotel and couldn't walk for the next few days.

Brett set up a training camp in Ishigaki, a lush tropical island, to prep for the Gamagori race, which was five weeks away. I couldn't run for three weeks and did a mind-numbing amount of water running. My race plan was to swim and ride my hardest and do the best I could on the run. If my foot really hurt, I would just call it. The people at New Balance said they'd pay a quarter of my salary if I started the race. I'd get my full salary if I finished.

Loretta, who'd finished second in Ishigaki, flew back to Australia to be with her family. After she left, I felt like I didn't have to put on a strong front for her sake. Living alone in a tiny hostel room, where I spent countless hours watching sumo matches on a small, grainy TV screen, I sank into a deep depression. All of my emotions and physical pain met in a wicked maelstrom. Part of my anxiety came from my inability to shake the feeling that I was living a lie because I hadn't had the courage to be openly gay. My good friend and training partner back in Boulder, Pat Brown, called me soon after I arrived in Japan to tell me that coming out was the best decision he'd ever made. I was happy for him and encouraged by his confidence and experience, but I still struggled with the notion of revealing my own truth. Pat's call made me realize how far away I was from that place of true self-acceptance. I'd been discreet in my relationships, but I'm sure a lot of people, including Brett, knew. I didn't want being gay to be a stumbling block to realizing my ambitious triathlon dreams, but what I didn't realize was that I would have to fully embrace who I really was before I could achieve my best results.

"I am so amazed at the fragility of my mind and of my emotions," I wrote in an e-mail to Brett.

> Confidence in myself is hard earned and so easily lost. This is a weakness that I really want to change. . . . This injury prevents me from fully throwing myself into the thing that I love and that really gets me down. But I will throw myself into the things that I can and that is swimming, biking, getting my foot healthy and my mind strong, and listening to you, as I know you understand me, god knows

> how, and can help. . . . Thanks for being patient with me right now, I promise you I will do my best to get back on track, physically, emotionally and mentally.

True to his tough-love form, Brett responded by telling me I didn't have to "do a damn thing to please anybody." But I had a choice to make, he said: "As to the life stuff, again, it is an easy decision—stand up or sit down. I am not a sit down guy, never have been never will be so I won't tolerate those around me being one. You have nothing to be ashamed of, far from it, so move on kid, wasting time on such things is not productive."

Brett wouldn't tolerate me being scared or fragile, and when he told me I needed to stop hiding and be proud of who I was, I knew exactly what he was getting at—he didn't care that I was gay, but he insisted that I own my fears as a step in overcoming my demons. Brett proved to be a steward of not just my athletic dreams but also my overall well-being, and with his support and M's compassionate care, the dark veil of self-doubt began to lift.

Two days before I was set to leave for Gamagori, I got a massive toothache. I was in absolute agony. I got up in the middle of the night and woke up Brett and his wife to ask if they had any painkillers. Brett and Fiona had nothing to help, and I went back to my room, where I lay awake with a throbbing jaw until morning. I found an interpreter associated with ITU and begged her to take me to a dentist. There was much confusion among the three of us as I pointed into my mouth. The dentist was convinced that the culprit was not the tooth I was pointing to but the tooth right next to it. He started a root canal on the tooth but couldn't finish because his office was closing. My translator told him I was leaving the next morning, and he said I would have to find a dentist in Gamagori to finish the job. He gave me a few prescriptions, but I had no idea what any of the drugs were, so I took Tylenol instead, which did nothing to dull the pain. It felt like someone was operating a jackhammer on my face.

The next morning, I boarded the flight, and the air pressure inside the cabin magnified the throbbing pain. I thought I was going to pass out from the pain—it was like nothing I'd ever felt. I landed in Gamagori and struggled to keep it together until my dentist appointment the next morning. Loretta's dad, Russell, came with me.

The dentist looked in my mouth and asked why I had the start of a root canal in a normal tooth. He took X-rays and saw that I had an abscess that needed immediate attention. Five hours of work later, the dentist said I needed to be extremely vigilant in protecting my mouth from germs because the abscess was still open and highly vulnerable to viral infection. I knew that the race swim was in a motorboat stadium with truly dubious water quality (given that hundreds of boats release fuel and other debris into a stagnant body of water).

I called Brett and asked him what to do. We decided that one race wasn't worth the very real threat of serious illness, so I didn't start. Loretta ended up winning, but it was a bittersweet day, as she broke her foot during the race.

I went back to Switzerland for training camp and had my teeth worked on some more (the whole ordeal wouldn't be totally resolved until after I got back to Boulder in November). The previous month had been miserable, but I had gained a new appreciation for my health and channeled my energy into a solid four-week training block. At the end of it, I was running better than ever.

One afternoon, Brett had me tackle a brutally tough treadmill workout: 10 × 1 km at 20 km per hour (4:50–5:00 per mile). On the second one, I felt a flare in my plantar fascia that was growing distinctly more intense with every stride. I was sure that if I continued, it would tear. I knew my body and breathlessly told Brett, "I'm in so much pain and am going to tear my plantar fascia if I keep running." He said I had two choices: Do 6 more intervals at 19 kph (slightly slower) or do 1 more at 21 kph (a little faster).

I was in agony and wanted to follow my gut and stop, but I knew that if I stopped, I would lose Brett's respect, which I'd worked hard to earn. I also knew that if he was in an especially intolerant mood, he'd tell me to pack my bags. I wasn't tough enough; I didn't have what it takes, he'd say. So I increased the speed on the treadmill and hung on for dear life. Within 30 seconds, I felt the muscle under my foot tear in a hot blast. I mustered every ounce of will to stay upright long enough to turn off the treadmill before collapsing onto the ground in a flood of tears. If I'd just honored my instincts, I could have avoided this massive setback. I was pissed and devastated that I'd allowed myself to get detoured, creating a longer road to full recovery.

I had one month to heal before the 2002 Edmonton World Cup race, which I desperately wanted to win—it would be the exclamation point on my 2001 world title win there. I "ran" in the pool for three weeks and focused on building my swim and bike fitness. I made sure to maintain my race weight despite the fact that I couldn't run. I knew this would be important. When I got back to running, I would be in the best form possible and increase my chances of getting right back to winning, or at least racing as strong as I could. I ran for the first time a few days before the race and was relieved when my foot held up okay without any pain.

I was at about 80 percent of my peak fitness when I flew to the 2002 Edmonton World Cup race in July. I was nervous because it had been two months since I'd raced, but I was grateful to be healthy enough to start. I didn't have a great swim, but I worked hard on the bike and started the run 2:30 behind the leaders—Sheila, Becky Lavelle, and Barb. I was able to catch them all, passing Barb in the last 100 meters to take the win. I posted the fastest run split of the day, and it felt good to be back on top.

Careful not to tempt reinjury in training, I won four more World Cup races by the end of August and was second in Hamburg. Despite the string of strong results, I was finding it harder and harder to go into tough workouts with much motivation or focus. The old Siri would attack a 400s track session with "Let's get fired up and get it done!" gusto. The new Siri was barely holding on. The countdown clock on my pro career was ticking. I remember one particular workout: 6 × 8 minutes hard on the bike, followed by a fast 10-km treadmill run. It was brutal but one of the best sessions of my life because I knew it was one of the last times I'd be doing it. My body was telling me, *Enough.* I couldn't keep weight on and was sleeping an average of two to three hours a night. There was no doubt that I was going to keep giving 100 percent as long as I was racing, but I was losing the desire to put in the necessary effort.

Brett had stopped coming to all my sessions, and that was hard because having him at my treadmill and bike workouts brought out the best in me. I think he was growing increasingly annoyed that I was training back home in Boulder part of the year, which meant I wasn't blindly obeying his demands 100 percent of the time. And I didn't share his opinion that I should hate—not befriend—my biggest competitors so that I could harness that contempt on race day. He continued to see my relationship with Loretta as a marker of dependency, of frailty. I couldn't help but feel that he wasn't as invested as he had been, and his detachment made me crave an outside lifeline even more.

Mentally, I was in a place of limbo, knowing that I wanted to retire after the 2002 ITU world championships on November 9 in Cancún but still trying to keep my head in the game. It was a struggle.

I went to Mexico with mixed emotions. I drew confidence from my five-race winning streak, but I felt such intense psychological burnout. I had a terrible swim, ended up killing myself on the bike to catch up, and neglected to eat or drink anything—a rookie mistake. I ran for my life and don't remember the last two laps. I crossed the finish line in 13th place and collapsed into the arms of Loretta, who had finished 12 seconds ahead of me in 12th place.

That was it. My pro career was over.

I knew in my heart of hearts that the time had come. While it wasn't the result I wanted to go out on, my disappointment mingled with utter relief. It was like coming up for air after a deep, deep dive—seeing the glimmer of light at the surface made every cell of my body buzz in anticipation of relief.

Loretta, whose opinion I valued more than anyone's, supported my decision. "What better time to get out than when you're number one?" she said. It was well and truly time. If anything, I'd hung on too long. She could see I was ready to start the next chapter of my life.

I wrote Brett a letter. I told him that he had not only helped me achieve my wildest dreams in the sport but given me invaluable insights into myself. He once told me, "You have a coach who knows why you become good and knows how to stop you from fucking that up." It was absolutely true. Under Brett, I had reached the pinnacle of the sport—and in the journey found myself. He was a maestro at getting his athletes to understand their motives, weaknesses, fears, and desires and then leveraging that self-awareness to help them unlock the little piece of magic buried deep within. He led me down a path of athletic breakthrough and personal transformation by bolstering my self-belief. For those gifts, I will be eternally grateful to Brett Sutton.

He was disappointed, and I'm sure he saw the decision as an act of simply giving up, of caving to the pressure and pain, but I wouldn't be deterred. It was a dream exit scenario to leave when I was ranked number one in the world. I had proven I wasn't a one-season sensation and would step away on my own terms. I was 33 and excited for a new direction.

I began sharing my retirement plans and was met by the same reaction time and again. *What are you thinking? The Olympics are coming up in two years; are you crazy? It's your second chance at a medal! You're on top of the world—why walk away now? There are more world titles to be won, more paychecks to be cashed!*

But I couldn't fathom one more day of putting my body and mind through the rigors of it all. I couldn't do it anymore. I was ready to move on.

That's not to say I didn't let the detractors get into my head. There were moments when I questioned my decision. During one such moment, just under a year after the Cancún race, I e-mailed Loretta. The subject line read "my chances":

> Loretta,
>
> In all seriousness, do you think, considering how far I have let myself fall, there could ever be a chance I could get back into it? Ever be a chance I could get my swim back, my bike back, my run back, enough to race respectably well? . . . I think it's too late, I have let myself go too much . . . but if I thought there was any chance at all, I may try.

The next morning I woke up to this response:

> Take a trip to the shrink, not the pool, not the track, not the cycle circuit. The fucking loony dr. might help. What are you talking about? You were fucking HATING it. End of story. You think it's gonna be different just because you have had time out, it will be harder. . . . I am not trying to be horrible, I just can't fucking understand you and it frustrates me.
>
> You retired as world no. 1, on a winning streak of World Cups . . . and guess what, reality check, you had had enough. Training with me or not, you were hating it! You are 35 next bday, give me a good reason why you want to go back and I might stop going on . . . but simply

missing it is bullshit, cause of course you are gonna miss it whether you retire now or when you are fucking 60!

If it is the Olympic dream that is eating you up have a look at your selection races again. They are meant for swimmers and you have about 7 of them in the US, making your job even harder to qualify for the games, plus they [the selection committee] can't stand you so you would have to win them all to get even a look in. As your best friend I will be with you no matter what you decide, and yes I think you could be good again but in all honesty you would have to improve your swim even more than you did with Brett in order to be up with your USA front runners, cause they are running quick and biking great as well as swimming like fish. So do you want to compete or do you want to win? Big difference.

For God's sake, either do it or let it fucking go. Get on with life. There is so much ahead of you that doesn't involve triathlon but you have to decide to let it go. Now that you are done all you are thinking of is the great times, which is how it should be, but it doesn't change all the shit you went through to get that. Stop and think of how much you hated Spain, your last camp.

And in my books you would ruin a great champion who retired at the perfect time, but that is me looking at it from where I stand and it isn't my decision.

Loretta was right—there was no turning back.

8

REINVENTED

ONE OF THE HARDEST PARTS of retiring was accepting that I would never again be so physically fit. Nailing a workout or having a strong race performance made me feel like Superwoman. I had invested 10 years of blood, sweat, and tears to get to that place. I missed the feeling of pure exhaustion at the end of a hard day's work—the ache in my legs that meant I'd given it my all. And I missed the thrill of racing hard and laying it all on the line. The desire to be the best I could be every second of every day was still there even though my principal outlet no longer existed. How would I satiate that hunger moving forward?

I also missed Brett. It was hard not to have him in my life in the same way, and I felt a distinct void because he understood me like no one else. He'd been my greatest mentor, but I also still felt a little wounded by the way things had eroded toward the end. I couldn't help but think that maybe I would have wanted to hang in a little longer if our relationship had been as positive as it had been in 2001.

I was also heartbroken to leave Annie and Loretta, who were family to me. With Loretta especially, I felt an intense separation anxiety. We had been through so much together, and we leaned heavily on each other as training partners—she is one of the toughest, most courageous, determined, and dangerous athletes the sport has ever seen—and best friends. Part of me felt like I was letting her down, but Loretta understood my motivations better than anyone, and her emphatic support was what ultimately gave me the confidence to make the leap into retirement.

Despite the initial anxieties (and a feud with USAT's Libby Burrell to collect a $10,000 results-based season bonus, which I ultimately lost because I retired in November, a month shy of the end of the calendar year), there was tremendous peace in retiring. I had pushed into the unknown and faced my demons. I had proven to myself that no challenge was insurmountable. I could not only overcome—I could *thrive*. I knew I had a good head on my shoulders, and I felt comfortable in my own skin. The future was wide open, and I was nearly giddy with anticipation.

I had created a bit of a nest egg from racing, and, using money from the sale of the Worcester townhouse M had helped me buy, I'd bought and sold a series of properties in Boulder, all getting me closer to buying my dream home on Wonderland Lake in 2003.

Two months retired, I went to Australia for Loretta's wedding to her high school sweetheart, Brad Jones. I was going to spend two weeks with Annie and Loretta and would see Brett as well, and I didn't know how it would feel to be immersed again in that world. They would be training all day, just as we'd all done together for years. Would I feel depressed and regretful? Or would I be content with my decision to leave? When I got there and Annie and Loretta said they were heading out for a full day of training, I told them I'd see them for dinner and spent a leisurely day Rollerblading and lounging at the beach. I was more than okay sitting it out—my training drive had clearly been blunted. I was also there for the Luke Harrop Memorial Race and was excited to be on the sidelines, cheering on my friends and honoring Luke's life. I felt no desire to be out on the racecourse. I'd had the courage to follow my instincts, and it was an encouraging sign that I was headed in the right direction.

Back home, I began visiting a minimal-security female prison in Denver to speak to the women there. I could see myself in some of these women who had felt demoralized and fearful for so long and wanted to tell them they could change the direction of their lives. *You can rewrite the script.*

My goal was to find out what every person's talent or passion was and encourage her to pursue it. One woman, whose name was Precious, had an incredible voice. After some encouragement, she sang a few lines, and it blew me away. I told her when she was released, she should pursue a singing career. When I was leaving, the warden pulled me aside. "Do you have any idea why Precious is in here?" she asked. "Let's just say you would not want to find yourself alone with her in a dark alley." It rattled me, but I was resolute in my mission of giving other people hope that they too could take control of their story.

Lynn Oski, Yoli Casas, Jack Ralston, and Brett Sutton had played such key roles in helping me change the narrative. I knew I wanted to do the same for other people. And then, in the summer of 2003, I received an e-mail that helped turn my intention into reality.

"I know this is a weird question," started the note. "But now that you're retired, would you consider coaching me?"

Jill Savege was a Canadian pro with whom I had shared the World Cup podium many times, and I had a lot of respect for her as a fierce competitor. In addition to the 2003 ITU world championship, she was targeting the Pan American Games as well as the 2004 Olympics in Athens. I immediately knew that I wanted to say yes, but I responded that she had to be willing to move from Penticton to Boulder. She was all in and wanted to get to work right away. All of a sudden, it seemed like everything I'd done in the sport had been preparing me for this new journey. Every lesson I'd learned through equally spectacular successes and failures, my curiosity about how other athletes trained, my innate empathy for others and passion for helping people get the best out of themselves—it was all pointing to this path. I'd found my calling.

My requirement that Jill move to Boulder was based on two core beliefs: Athletes make the most significant gains while training in a squad environment, which I would create, and athletes benefit tremendously by having their coach at training sessions. I had learned the value of both of these things from personal experience. When I closed myself off to prepare for the Sydney Trials, I was miserable and choked on race day. Once I embraced my support team, I became successful. I learned from everyone around me, not just my coaches.

I was always observing every single person on Brett's squad, even the long-course athletes. That is what makes the team environment so powerful—the exposure to different approaches and outcomes. My teammates taught and motivated me, and I also wanted to push harder when Brett was standing there intently watching over me. If something was off, Brett could see it right away and correct mistakes. He relied on his experience as a former thoroughbred horse trainer to read the nuanced body language of his squad members and respond. You can't do that if you're not there with your athlete.

I had been in periodic touch with Brett since retiring, and I reached out to get his blessing to start coaching athletes. He was supportive—I think he could see how much I'd learned about myself in my own journey and knew I was passionate about helping others achieve the same things. But he also said he wasn't sure I had thick enough skin for it. Athletes will come and go, he warned, and, knowing how emotionally invested I'd be in each person, he questioned whether I'd be able to handle that.

Word got around Boulder that I was looking to build my squad, and in addition to Jill, I took on Australian Olympian Matt Reed; a Swedish pro named Marcin Wedlarski; Americans Courtney Benningson and Amory Rowe, one of my former players from the Princeton lacrosse team; and a few age groupers. My good friend Annie Emmerson trained with us when she visited, and other Boulder-based pros like Cam Brown, Chris Legh, and Luke Bell would drop in for some workouts.

My coaching style was—and is—a hybridized reflection of my influences and experiences. I incorporated training techniques and principles I learned from Jack and Brett, but I related more to Yoli's encouraging and positive energy (the smiling assassin approach). I wanted to make training fun, but I also had high expectations. I got annoyed if someone wasn't paying attention or seemed to be wasting the group's time. That was Coach Spellman's imprint. She had high expectations but always made me feel like she cared about me as a person. That's the balance I wanted to strike from the very beginning. Loretta was also a tremendous teacher in every way, and I gleaned a lot of knowledge and insight from her.

As a coach, I still had the opportunity to learn a lot from Loretta. After 10 years with Brett, she decided it was time for a change and came to stay with me in Boulder. We'd sit down at the dinner table each Sunday and talk through her training plans for the week ahead, and she'd explain the purpose of specific sessions and why a certain workout gave her an edge physically or mentally. She also valued my input, and we collaborated for the next eight months on her training plan of attack for the 2004 Olympics. I was there for every session.

Around the same time that Loretta came to Boulder, Olympic hopeful Susan Williams approached me about also training her. Susan had been racing for the national team at the World Cup level for more than seven years and was ranked as the sixth American but hadn't yet qualified for Team USA. She had targeted the 2000 Games in Sydney but found out she was pregnant just a few days before the trials. Four years later, she wanted another shot at her Olympic dream.

It was the middle of winter in Boulder, and the qualifying race was in April. I told Susan that if she was truly serious, we would need to go to California for at least two months for focused training in milder temperatures. She couldn't have any distractions—her infant (aptly named Sydney) and husband would have to stay home in Colorado. Unless she could commit to that, I was unwilling to help her. A goal of that magnitude demanded that kind of sacrifice, I explained. She looked at me like I was kind of a maniac and then said thanks, but no thanks.

But a couple of days later, she called me and said, "I can't believe I'm saying this, but I'm in." Her mom had agreed to come help take care of the baby, and her husband would hold down the fort in her absence.

"We leave in a week," I told her.

The situation showed me how sincerely passionate and focused I was in my new mission. I was ready and willing to abruptly relocate my life for months and devote everything to helping my athlete realize her goal. *Wow, I must really want to do this—and do it right.*

We set up camp in San Luis Obispo in central California and went to work. We got to the first qualifier, a World Cup race in Honolulu, and she didn't make the cut. There was one remaining qualifying event a couple of months later, and Susan was in a battle with Laura Reback (now Bennett) for the spot. All Susan had to do was finish before Laura in the race. We were both ecstatic when Susan came in third and Reback was fifth. Susan hadn't been on anyone's radar since returning from pregnancy, and it felt incredible as a rookie coach to have her achieve her goal and surprise everyone in the process.

Susan's training for the Olympics was structured vastly differently than Loretta's, and I went to Athens wondering which approach would produce the best result. Ranked fourth in the world, Jill Savage was considered a medal contender, but after a fairly short stint of working together, we had a strong difference of opinion and parted ways before the Games.

In addition to my support roles for Loretta and Susan, I had been hired by NBC as a commentator for the Olympic triathlon and field hockey coverage. During my interview with NBC Olympics coverage head David Neal in New York City, I mentioned I'd coached field hockey at Princeton, and his eyes lit up. They were having a hard time finding knowledgeable commentators for the planned 1,210 hours of coverage so were eager to have me on board to cover both sports. They brought all of us rookie analysts to New York for a seminar and coached us on the importance of doing our homework ("Call the coaches, talk to the athletes, explain the rules") and telling a clear, concise but engaging story. They showed us videos of people doing it wrong and people getting it right. They wanted astute insights and genuine honesty in our commentary, not banal cheerleading. They also told us they had exceptionally high standards and expectations. This was, after all, the Olympics. It had been so long since my field hockey days at Brown that I spent hours catching up on the rules, current stats, players, and coaches. It was exhilarating to be in the company of female announcers I idolized and respected as trailblazers in a male-dominated world—former tennis player Mary Carillo and track and field star Carol Lewis. I was fortunate to get to know both of these paragons and learned a great deal from both of them as well as from sports broadcasting legend Al Trautwig, who shared the commentator booth for triathlon with me.

I was nervous but drew some confidence from my prior experience in the broadcasting booth. In 2003, I'd been hired by NBC Sports to call the action of the Life Time Fitness Triathlon, a big-money Olympic-distance race, with veteran sports commentator Ted Robinson. (I went on to do this for four consecutive years). The pro race featured a unique format that had the women starting in front of the men, and the entire field competed for the $500,000 prize purse (first place won $200,000)—a significant amount of money for a triathlon purse, even by today's standards. (The Ironman World Championship prize purse is currently $650,000, with the male and female winners each getting $125,000.) I remember being so nervous for that first gig that I couldn't get my knees to stop trembling—thankfully, they weren't on camera. My biggest concern was finding the right amount of energy and enthusiasm without being over the top.

Commentating challenged and captured me like racing did. You could do everything in your power to be totally prepared, having left no stone unturned, but you still had to roll with the punches on race day and bring your sharpest game. It was inspiring to watch a true professional like Ted Robinson at his craft, and he made me feel comfortable from the get-go. The show's producers weren't afraid to offer constructive criticism, which I appreciated as a person who's always striven for self-improvement.

Because of my NBC commitment in Athens, I couldn't be with Susan very much, but we would talk every day. The other two women representing the USA were Sheila Taormina, a gold-medal swimmer who had been on the 2000 Olympic triathlon team and finished sixth, and Barb Lindquist, ranked number one in the world in 2003 and 2004. They were two of the biggest stars in the sport. Susan would call me in tears, saying USAT was catering to Sheila and Barb and that she was taking a backseat to their schedules and needs. I understood what she was feeling, thinking back on my experience as an alternate in Sydney. I did my best to calm her down and told her she couldn't afford to waste her energy worrying about anyone else. She needed to focus on her own race.

The Olympic triathlon took place on August 24, 2004. As anticipated, Loretta, Sheila, and Barb took early control in the swim, and then Loretta and Sheila extended their lead on the bike. They continued to work together at the front while Susan, who also had a great swim, and Barb fought hard to keep them in striking distance. By the final bike lap, Loretta had managed a break from Sheila, and she started the 10K run with a 20-second lead over the three Americans and 2.5 minutes ahead of the main chase pack, led by Aussie Kate Allen, who was an Austrian citizen. Loretta maintained the lead on the run until the last 100 meters, when Kate Allen blasted by her to break the tape for gold. Loretta finished seven seconds later for silver, and an ecstatic Susan held on for bronze.

Talk about a thrilling race—my best friend led from the start, looking like she was all but guaranteed gold, and my athlete was in podium contention. Co-commentator Al Trautwig could see what a big moment that was for me, and he told me to have the last word after the top women came through the finish. My response just tumbled out of my mouth: "Well, Al, Kate Allen has won it, but the real gold-medal performance belongs to Loretta Harrop!"

Right away I worried that I'd made a major gaffe, but the producers actually applauded me for my honesty (and I was invited back as an analyst for the 2008 Games in Beijing). Some people said I was biased toward my friend and unfairly downplayed Kate, but Loretta had put together an incredible race worthy of that top step on the podium. The 10 years Brett spent working with Loretta was a huge part of what she achieved that day. I was over the moon that both Loretta and Susan walked away as Olympic medalists. And my plan for Susan had worked beautifully.

Brett knew that an Olympic medal had been my dream, and in 2006 I received a totally unexpected e-mail from him asking me if I'd consider a bid for the 2008 Games in Beijing. He wrote:

> I have no doubt that now that you can fail and not be in fear of it, then it is totally achievable. The training would not be trouble at all, some people are programmed for it. . . . It's this simple: Do I want one last chance to go to the Olympics? Does it mean something to me? Is there a hole that feels unfinished? And then, can I put 18 months of this life into making it happen? If the answer is yes, then you got your answer. If it's a hand on the heart I could not give a fuck, then you have one there too.

I was flattered that Brett thought I still had it in me to compete at that level, but I knew deep down I couldn't possibly go down that road. I told him that while a part of me was exhilarated by the prospect, I was happy being retired. I reminded him of something he'd said to me before: "The sign of a true champion is one who can retire and stay retired." I hadn't been in a pool in two years, and I'd been on my bike no more than five times in that same time span. "I don't feel any competitive fire anymore and, therefore, I think the champ has gone," I wrote. "That fire lies in just wanting my life to be as good as it can be in different ways."

I also had a verbal offer from NBC to do the Olympics commentary for triathlon and field hockey again, and I wasn't going to forgo that opportunity. I was excited to do even better the second time around. I told him I felt satisfied with my pro career as it stood, "mostly because it wasn't about the sport, it was all about what I learned about myself, my own capabilities and the fact that I was a hell of a lot stronger than I ever gave myself credit for." And I thanked him again for showing me the way to that personal discovery. Racing wasn't just about me anymore, and I liked it that way. Now the glory and gratification came from seeing my athletes achieve their goals. I realized just how committed I was to my coaching.

9

BELIEVE

IN 2005, LORETTA WAS TRAINING with me in Boulder when a 24-year-old basketball player turned ITU racer named Mirinda Carfrae came to a couple of her track sessions and swim workouts. I had done a few of the same races as "Rinny" and was always impressed by her work ethic, and seeing her again only reinforced my opinion that she was intensely focused and a tremendously hard worker. At 5 feet 3 inches and 115 pounds, she had the lean but powerful physique of an incredible athlete. When Rinny, who had represented Australia at the ITU world championships every year since 2001 (she captured silver in 2002 and 2003), left her coach of five years and was looking for someone new to work with, Loretta thought we would be a fantastic fit and encouraged me to recruit her. But it wasn't my style to go chasing after an athlete, no matter how much I wanted to work with her. If she was interested in joining up with me, then she could reach out.

But Loretta persisted, saying Rinny wouldn't come to me—I'd have to extend myself to her. In early January 2006 I was in Australia visiting Loretta and decided to contact Mirinda. I knew I would have a hard time being very forward in person, so I decided to send her an e-mail describing my training philosophy and making a case for what we could achieve together:

> I believe that you have what it takes to be a true champion Mirinda, a force to be reckoned with in every race you line up at. I know that I have what it takes to bring that out of you, and to help you get to a point where every race you do, whether you feel crappy or great, you can dominate . . . yeah, this requires an incredible amount of hard work and commitment, but so worth it in the end.
>
> I don't coach just to have a job, I don't coach for the hell of it. I coach like I raced . . . wanting to be the very best that I can be and achieve incredible success in every "project" I take on. Your dreams become my dreams . . . my heart and soul goes into wanting to make my athletes the best that they can possibly be. In your case, you have the ability, in my opinion, to be one of the best in the world, but it will take a magic combination and a hell of a lot of hard work, but I know it can be yours.

Rinny responded and said she was interested in talking more. I suggested we meet at Loretta's house. I knew she looked up to Loretta and that it couldn't hurt to have Loretta in her ear saying, "You need Siri as your coach!" The morning of our meeting, I wrote a second impassioned email to Mirinda. I didn't want to miss anything. There was a lot I wanted to say.

From the beginning, I saw in Rinny an athlete who could stand out from all the rest in both long-distance and short-distance races. I was convinced that my programs could make Rinny a long-distance world champion and a consistent winner on the short-course circuit. I also believed I knew what it would take to get to the Olympics. Having trained under Brett, who has produced multiple world champions and studying what has worked for myself and the athletes around me, I possessed an unwavering confidence required to coach a champion. I made a bold promise: I would help Rinny win the long-distance world championship, get her on the Olympic team, and make her into a dominant triathlete at every distance. It came with a guarantee:

> I want you to win for me as much as you want to win for yourself. Give me 3 months of your total commitment, your complete dedication. If after 3 months you are not happy . . . you move on. No questions asked. I won't twist your arm, but if you want to win a world championship and race at the Olympics, come with me now.
>
> Siri

We had our meeting, and I was beyond thrilled when Rinny asked how soon we could start. (She later said that the words in my e-mail jumped off the page at her.) I had a strong feeling that we were going to accomplish something special. I had no idea what it would be or how we were going to do it, but I just knew it was the start of something extraordinary. I spent an entire weekend working on her training plan for the following week, poring over every detail. My adrenaline was racing as I anticipated what came next.

My goal was to build up Rinny's strength by training her to race the half-Ironman like a back-to-back Olympic race. She had to learn how to go fast for a longer period of time. The approach was very much trial and error, and I adjusted her training to get us closer and closer to her being able to hold that same Olympic pace effort over 70.3 miles. I always took into consideration what she thought about the program and made adjustments based on her feedback. She came to Boulder for six weeks to train with the squad, which included American ITU racer Sarah True (formerly Groff), US pro Mary Beth Ellis, Canadian Lauren Groves (formerly Campbell), and aspiring pro Mary Miller. (Mary is the reason I call Rinny "Vincent," a nickname that has stuck through the years. The first time Mary and Rinny were at the same workout, Mary thought I was calling Rinny by the name Vinnie. We all had a good laugh, and Vinnie morphed into Vincent.) I attended every workout and focused on building up her self-belief. When she nailed a hard run session, I made sure to emphasize that what she'd just accomplished was world class. She needed to believe that she belonged among the best. I knew we were just scratching the surface of her ability, and it was my job to keep chipping away to let the champion emerge. I began to earn her trust by proving that time and again, I had her best interests in mind, even when she didn't understand my reasoning or agree on the course of action. There was good reason why I structured her workouts a certain way and why we targeted specific races. Her full confidence that I knew what was best for her wasn't automatic or immediate, but it wasn't long before it began to take root.

Rinny did a few World Cup races that season (2006), but the real focus was her 70.3 debut in St. Croix. She was completely unknown on the half-Iron circuit but stormed in and ran a 1:22 half-marathon on a hot and hard course to set a new St. Croix record of 4:30:13. We were both blown away. To this day, we look back at that race in amazement at what a remarkable debut it was. She displayed her mental toughness and ability to sit right at the upper limit of her pain threshold for hours—two qualities that distinguish long-course stars. It was an immense confidence booster, and two weeks later, she won a 70.3 in Baja, Mexico, and then placed third at the Ironman 70.3 world championship in Clearwater, Florida.

After she started winning 70.3 races, Rinny began talking about Ironman. I was adamant that she was too young and that Ironman racing would take too much out of her both physically and mentally. I also needed the time to learn and prepare—I had to be ready for that huge step, too. Certainly, there were a lot of valuable lessons from our shared Olympic and 70.3 experience that we could transfer to Ironman training, but neither of us wanted to rush the process. There would be plenty of time to solve that particular puzzle.

A month before the 2007 Ironman 70.3 world championship, I held a two-week training camp in Kona. I watched the Hawaii Ironman, and I was able to pick the brains of Ironman legends like Scott Tinley, Mark Allen, Paula Newby-Fraser, and Wendy Ingraham. I had so many questions.

Rinny arrived in Clearwater for 70.3 world's ready to prove that her podium finish in 2006 wasn't a fluke. She didn't have a single sponsor, and when her new manager approached one well-known triathlon brand, he was quickly rebuffed. In a flawless performance, Rinny captured her first world title in 4:07:25, a new women's record at the distance. As the champion, she was awarded entry into the 2008 Ironman world championship, and we decided to defer it to the 2009 race. We needed more time. *Triathlete* magazine named Rinny the 2007 Ironman 70.3 Triathlete of the Year. In 2008, she would win four more 70.3s all around the world.

I had been carrying on a long-distance relationship with a woman who lived in Los Angeles, and, completely lovestruck, I decided in 2008 to move to California. I set everything up to train there and presented my plan to my squad of 15 athletes. I assured them that I was as committed as ever to the team and that they would love the camp environment in Los Angeles, but only two were willing to leave Boulder: Rinny and a Mexican triathlete named Marcela Miramontes. I was disappointed because I'd always been loyal and kept the faith in my athletes through the good times and the rough patches, and I expected the same in return. We were supposed to be equally invested. Brett had been right: Maybe I didn't have the stomach for coaching. It was a great test of resiliency.

I quickly sold my house on Wonderland Lake, gave much of my furniture and other belongings away, put my two dogs—Whoopi and my beloved St. Bernard, Billy—and cat, Gracie, in the back of the car, and drove to West Hollywood. Leaving M was hard, especially because she was skeptical of my new relationship. I moved into a tiny apartment with my girlfriend, and our lives began to merge, including financially when I added a second name to my credit cards and the title of the house I later bought.

I could have told Rinny I was moving to the moon and she would have been okay with it because she trusted that I was fully committed to her. There was no reason to think otherwise. In 2009, our goal was a strong 70.3 season, and she won five of the six half-Ironman races she started (she finished second at St. Croix). She was successfully building the mileage on her rides and runs and logging more double-run days. The progression was steady and methodical. When July arrived, we started ramping up her Ironman-specific training. I didn't want to train Rinny the way everyone else was approaching Ironman—it had to feel instinctively right to me. There was much work to be done with her swim. She needed to increase her efficiency and strength on the bike. She lacked an efficient pedal stroke and wasn't as strong as she should be on the climbs, so we addressed both weaknesses. I asked her to do things differently and really took her out of her comfort zone.

We went to Kona in October 2009, cautiously confident, and approached the race as a massive learning opportunity. Rinny had never run a marathon before, but we trusted the work we'd done. She swam a 58:45, biked a 5:14:18—nowhere near her actual ability because she was nervous about simply going the distance—and ran a 2:56:51. In her very first Ironman, she clocked 9:13:59, finishing in second place and establishing a new run course record, which had been set by winner Chrissie Wellington of Britain the previous year. (Chrissie, who was coached by Brett Sutton, would go on to win a total of four Ironman world titles and retire undefeated in the Ironman distance. She still owns the Iron-distance world record.) We couldn't be happier about a Kona podium in Rinny's Ironman debut, but we also knew she could go even faster there. After Hawaii, we were confident we were on the right track.

The training in Los Angeles wasn't ideal—you had to drive to all the good riding and running routes—so I decided to set up a training compound in Borrego Springs in the Southern California desert, about two hours southeast of LA. It had been my dream to create my own triathlon training facility, and the woman I was living with owned a piece of land in Borrego Springs that I could use for such a purpose. I bought a prefabricated home and put it on the property, along with an aboveground 25-meter pool that we dubbed "the Fish Tank." I bought two used camper trailers, put bunk beds in one for athlete housing, and set up the other as a hangout space with a computer and spotty Wi-Fi (aka "the Internet café"). I rented space in town and created a minigym with two treadmills and some weights. I had promised Yoli that I would pay it forward after she'd helped me, and now I was in a position to do that by hosting and training deserving athletes at my new camp. I announced an application process and ended up inviting six South American athletes who couldn't afford to have me coach them. They just had to make it to camp, and from there I would take care of them.

Rinny was not a fan of our Borrego setup. It was desolate and could get hot as hell out there. She was roommates with Marcela, who spoke very little English, and outside of training, there was very little to do. She was lonely much of the time; she'd recently started dating her now husband, Tim O'Donnell, and it was hard being separated from him. But she hung tight with me. The target was the 2010 Ironman world championship, and we were laser focused. We were 100 percent committed to racing Ironman at the highest level, and we had to strike a balance of shared ideas that we both believed in. I wanted to use my knowledge and experience to put together an original plan that resonated with me—I wanted to take a chance. Rinny could have easily doubted it, but instead she was all in.

We arrived in Kona in 2010 fresh off a 70.3 winning streak (she won a total of five 70.3s that year), and we were optimistic and excited. On race morning, I slipped away to quickly use the restroom, and Shannon, Rinny's manager, came looking for me. The race announcer had just informed the crowd that the three-time Ironman world champion Chrissie Wellington would not be starting the race. (She had come down with an illness overnight.) The news threw Rinny into a bit of a tailspin. For a year, she'd known that Chrissie was the one to beat that day, and her race plan included the defending champion as an important reference point. She knew where she'd have to be in relation to Chrissie throughout the race to be in striking distance on the marathon. The possibility that she wouldn't be there to help drive the race dynamic had never occurred to her, and it felt like the rug had been pulled out from beneath her. Sitting by the pool at the King Kamehameha Hotel, I did my best to refocus her. "This changes nothing," I told her. "You will go out there and race your own race."

And that's exactly what she did. At 29 years old, Rinny posted the fourth-fastest time in the 32-year history of the race—8:58:36—and bettered her 2009 run course record with a 2:53:32 marathon. I could have burst with pride. I was proud of myself for taking that chance with her training plan and proud of her for believing in it and rising to the challenge so phenomenally. I had proven that a so-called short-course specialist could help Rinny win the world's most competitive long-course race. The fact that I was the first female coach to achieve this win was the icing on the cake.

On the heels of Rinny's 2010 success, Brett was quoted in an *Inside Triathlon* article about my squad: "She will be the best triathlon coach in America." I was officially living my dream.

While my professional life was soaring to new heights, my personal life was in absolute turmoil. Some very obvious red flags had been present since day one of my relationship, but now it had reached new depths of dysfunction. Yoli had tried to alert me early on, but I was wearing blinders and didn't want to see or hear it. So I'd cut her out of my life and dumped all my other detractor friends. But things had become so negative and toxic that I knew I needed to get out—I just didn't know how. Back in LA or at training camp in Borrego, I would go to work and be totally focused and engaged, and then I would go home and sleep because I was so depressed and couldn't deal with my imploding relationship. I wasn't exercising, which was out of character. I was disappointed in myself because I knew I was a strong and resilient person, but I had let myself feel weak and victimized. When I looked in the mirror, that lost, wounded little girl in the big Greenwich house stared back.

Rinny couldn't help but notice how miserable I was, and she told me that she was there for me if I needed her. I'd never shared details of my personal life with any of my athletes, and I felt that it was unprofessional to cross that line. But she said she knew something was very wrong; she cared about my well-being and happiness, and I should feel comfortable confiding in her. She had witnessed enough to understand the severity of the situation. I walked away from our conversation feeling supported and empowered to make a change. The next day, having made the decision to leave the relationship, I went for a run. I felt the cool air wash over me, and it felt like it was God saying, "Yep, that is exactly what I've been trying to tell you." And when I got home from work, I didn't take a long nap.

As part of our agreement to get my ex's name off the title of my home, I had to relinquish my training camp in Borrego for $1. In my estimation, I had built it up to a value of at least $350,000. But I just wanted to move on with my life. Financially, that meant starting over. Part of me wondered what the hell was going to happen to me, and another part of me knew I'd be okay. I stayed in California because I loved it there, and we were seeing some great results.

In 2011, Rinny finished on the podium in every race she entered (eight times) and won two 70.3s, but the outcome that carried the most weight that year for her was Kona. Chrissie was back, and Rinny wanted to prove she could win that race with her there. So when Rinny finished second to Chrissie at the 2011 Ironman world championship, it was a brutal pill to swallow. Rinny felt like she was at a crossroads and needed to really shake things up. She wanted to focus more on the bike and thought I wasn't using metrics enough in training. So in early 2012, she told me she was leaving. We were in Australia, and it was a very respectful discussion, but both of us walked away with heavy hearts. I was hurt, a bit ruffled, and disoriented. She was my North Star, and I had thought I was hers. How do you navigate in utter darkness?

Rinny linked up with another Boulder coach to help with her bike program, and she wrote her own swim and run plans. Meanwhile, Leanda Cave, who had finished third in Kona in 2011, had come to train with me the previous year, and she motivated the hell out of me. Of course I wanted to do well for Leanda, but I also wanted to show Rinny that I was an essential part of the winning recipe. I was going to prove it by helping Leanda win in Kona.

Leanda was a swift swimmer and strong cyclist; her weakness was her run at longer distances. We focused on improving her run mechanics and efficiency. She carried an electronic metronome during training runs in an effort to increase her stride rate. We did a lot of drills, hill repeats, and strength training to improve her power, speed, and endurance. Leanda was motivated to follow in Rinny's footsteps as far as her run progression, and she was relentless in training. She is tough as nails, and it was a matter of channeling her tenacity and drive for the most productive outcome, and maybe even a shot at the double world title—70.3 and Kona—which had never been done by a woman.

Except for a win at Escape from Alcatraz in 2012, Leanda's season had a fairly quiet start. She had raced the 70.3 world championship more than any other athlete, so experience was on her side, but the priority in her training had been Ironman. So we were more than pleasantly surprised when she put together a winning performance on that day. Leanda told finish-line reporters that she hadn't expected to win because many of her competitors had treated the race as their season goal. "This is not going to get in my head going to Kona," she said. "The Ironman is my goal, and I can't let this change the way I feel about going into Kona as my A race this year."

The preparation we did for Kona 2012 was vastly different than the training Rinny did for the same race. We had to zero in on the perfect recipe for Leanda, which again required taking a chance. I was on a mission.

I came up with every single possible scenario that could happen in Kona, and Leanda and I had a plan for all of them. Leanda swam in the front pack and rode toward the front of the entire bike leg until she was issued a drafting penalty. Caroline Steffen of Switzerland (one of Brett's athletes) was first onto the marathon, with American Mary Beth Ellis and Leanda 4 minutes in arrears. Leanda broke away from Mary Beth by the half-marathon mark for second place, but Rinny was closing fast as they entered the notoriously barren and hot Natural Energy Lab (the road temperature can get up to 115 degrees Fahrenheit) at about mile 15. Leanda and I had prepared for the moment when Rinny would catch her on the run. I was standing right there when Rinny came up behind Leanda, and I didn't know what to do with all the emotion I was feeling. I looked right into Leanda's face and gave her the look that said, *Don't you dare assume it's over*. They ran into the Energy Lab side by side, and because only the racers are allowed on this 3-mile section of the course, I stood there waiting for what felt like an eternity to see who would be the first to emerge back onto the Queen Kamehameha Highway. And then I saw a tall, lanky figure coming into sharper focus the closer it got. It was Leanda, and she was alone. I lost my mind and started screaming my head off. "I knew you could fucking do it!" I yelled. When Leanda got to me, she took off her fuel belt and tossed it at me. I read it as a sign that she was feeling so good, she didn't need it for the remaining 10K. The pass on Rinny gave Leanda the momentum and confidence she needed to take the lead from Caroline Steffen with about 3 miles to go. She won in 9:15:54 and became the first-ever female to win the world-title double in the same year.

It was one of the greatest days of my life. I was overjoyed for Leanda, and it was incredibly vindicating. Rinny had lost one of her water bottles on the bike and suffered a nutritional meltdown as a result but still held on for third place behind Caroline. After Kona, Rinny realized she needed a coach who could keep her from overtraining. She started working with a coach known for training ITU racers but soon realized what she was lacking had less to do with the program and more to do with the coach-athlete relationship.

In 2013, I decided to move back to Boulder. It's where my heart is, and I wanted to be near M again. Rinny heard that I was back in town, and she sent me an e-mail asking if we could talk. I was nervous but excited, wondering if she would ask to come back. She is a proud person, and I knew it took courage and humility on her part to reach out to me. I had made it known to the squad that when anyone left, they couldn't come back. But I couldn't completely close the door on Rinny. She came over to my house, and before we even started talking, we just cried. We acknowledged how hard the past couple of years had been, and Rinny said she knew that whatever we had was special and we had some unfinished business.

Before I could give her a definite yes, I had to talk to Leanda to make sure she was on board. I didn't think there would be a problem, and Leanda was supportive of Rinny rejoining the squad. She said they'd both won the world championship and understood the pressure. They'd gone through tough times, and they could still learn a lot from one another. It was a best-case scenario. I had great respect for Leanda for being so accepting, and I was happy to have Rinny back. In the end, her leaving was a positive thing because when she came back, she was more committed than ever. We both were.

Leanda had a hard road in 2013 as she grappled with a hamstring injury that she carried into Kona. I know it was tough finishing 13th after winning the previous year, especially because Rinny won Kona '13 in course-record fashion (she posted an astounding 8:52:14). At the finish line, Rinny credited her victory partly to me and said, "I just had one of those days where you don't hurt—I didn't know I had a performance like that in me." We had reclaimed our old magic.

Leanda ended up leaving the squad right after Kona, which I struggled with for some time. She never became any less important to me, but because she'd had a tougher year, I'm sure it must have felt like I had given Rinny more. I know deep down that I gave Leanda everything I had.

Rinny is far from a diva and has never expected special treatment. She knows that she has me in the important times, so I just have to organize my schedule so that I can be there for everyone as much as possible. If Rinny has a key session that I want to attend, I won't schedule a similar session for another athlete. Some athletes expect to be treated like the star, but Rinny doesn't. To be fair, if I've had an athlete for 10 years who's a four-time world champion, she has earned the right to get the best training time if I do have to juggle athletes' sessions. But it doesn't mean that she's getting more energy from me or that she's getting the special sauce while the others get leftovers.

Rinny and I have built a level of trust and communication that allows us to be completely transparent with one another. If she's traveling or I can't make it to a key session for some reason, she knows exactly what I'd be saying to her throughout a workout. If I say "Good job" to her and she doesn't think it's warranted, she'll tell me she doesn't want to hear it. We get through uncomfortable moments and become stronger as a team for it. Complete honesty isn't always easy, but God, it's powerful. We have an alchemy that comes from fully trusting, believing, and respecting one another. We are equally invested and put our entire lives into making our shared goals happen. That kind of commitment creates magic.

One of the best compliments I've ever received as a coach came from Brett after Kona 2014, when Rinny won for the third time and a few other women on my squad turned in breakthrough performances. "As I've said before," he wrote in his blog, "while Siri may gush 'you're awesome' a lot more than her previous coach, it's a cover for one of the deepest thinkers in our sport with an intellect equal to anyone in it."

I didn't need Brett to express that to believe it for myself, but the endorsement by my greatest mentor was gratifying beyond words. I'd proven that I could get results by doing things my way, in a singular style that reflected my unique values and insights.

I could be *me*, and it was more than enough.

10

GRATITUDE

DISMANTLING MY FEARS while building up self-belief allowed me to achieve great things in triathlon. But world titles—earned as either an athlete or a coach—are not what defines me. Not until I was married did I feel *whole*. The ability to love and be loved through a singular bond is not something I was ever certain I'd have in my life, and it satisfies my soul like nothing else. My relationship is deeply meaningful not just because of the extraordinary gifts it affords me every moment of the day but also because it is the ultimate reward after a long, zigzagging, and wearisome road to true self-acceptance. It is the award that trumps all awards.

As a kid, I was a textbook tomboy. I was tall and thin as a reed, athletic, kept my hair cropped short, and preferred shorts and sneakers to flouncy dresses. My friends ended up pooling their money to buy me my first bra, and even then I didn't really need it. I used to be mistaken for a boy all the time. This tendency grew increasingly mortifying the older I got, with one interaction in particular being especially traumatizing. As a preteen, I used to watch the soap opera *General Hospital,* and I was smitten with a handsome character named Robert Scorpio. M was married to Frank at the time, and he used his A-list connections to set up a tour of the set in Los Angeles. Getting ready to meet Robert Scorpio is my first memory of ever feeling self-conscious. When we arrived on the set, the actor who played Robert Scorpio—a guy named Tristan Rogers—walked over to greet us. He looked right at me with a warm smile, said, "Nice to meet you, son!" and gave me a firm pat on the back. I held it together long enough to get back to the car and then cried for hours. I was humiliated. I hadn't given my appearance much thought before, and I became keenly aware that girls are supposed to look a certain way. Pretty. Feminine. Demure. I felt none of those things.

During one stage in junior high, I grew my hair long and styled it obsessively. I went from one extreme to the other. I carried a curling iron in my backpack and would sneak into the auditorium—the only place where I could find privacy with an outlet—in the middle of the school day and curl my hair into Farrah Fawcett wings. I didn't wear makeup, but my clothes selection became important. I didn't dress super-girly, but I still wanted to be fashionable.

Every summer, my family went to Fire Island in New York with my mom's large extended family. In my memories of doing anything fun, especially when I was about 13, my cousin Stephi (my mom's brother's daughter) was always in the picture. I was fairly shy, and she, a total extrovert, brought me out of my shell. She opened my eyes to what it was like to draw comfort and happiness from true friendship. Stephi thought she would be the first one to kiss a boy, and she was wild with jealousy when I beat her to it. There was a gay beach on Fire Island, and we used to giggle at the men holding hands on the beach. Stephi would dare me to go lie down next to a naked sunbather and strike up a conversation with him. Afterward we would roll on the ground in hysterics.

My first boyfriend was a sweet surfer named Steve Debrun. I was 13 when we started dating. One night we were sitting out on the dock at Fire Island, kissing pretty innocently, when my hand grazed what Stephi and I called his "cornstalk." That became our inside joke. I always had casual boyfriends, but never any deep relationships. I used to be a kissing bandit—I was scared to do anything more.

In high school, when someone told me our gym teacher was gay, I didn't know what it meant. The kid explained that, in this case, it meant a girl who liked other girls. I was curious but didn't think too much about it.

I had sex for the first time when I was 21. He was a famous pro athlete who was significantly older and was a friend of Frank and M. He'd come to the house for long dinners. For years, I thought I was in love with him and that we'd get married one day. He actually said that to me—"I'm going to marry you someday." As an adoring teenager, I didn't understand that he didn't mean it literally. Even after M's divorce, he still made a point of visiting us, and I was adamant that he would be my first. I didn't intend to sleep with anyone else. Our sexual encounter was a disaster—not pleasurable in the least. My second time was with my college boyfriend, Eric, who waited a long time for me to go there. Eric, who was a starter on the hockey team, was super-dedicated and focused, and I felt safe with someone who cared as much about sports as I did. He was smart and encouraging, and I was comfortable with him. He was a gentleman and treated me like a queen. I wanted to enjoy it, I really did . . . but I just didn't.

At Brown, the lacrosse team captain, Suzanne, was a close friend. When Suzanne told me she was gay, I asked her a million questions about how she knew and what it was like being gay. She told me how she met her current girlfriend and how they were best friends and shared a lot in common and also had an undeniable mutual attraction. She had found someone who fulfilled all she wanted and needed in a gratifying and healthy relationship. After our conversation, I vowed that if I ever experienced that with another woman, I would have the courage to pursue those feelings. Still, there was no way I would tell anyone about this, except Suzanne, and she really educated me about what it meant to be gay, or at least made me question whether I might be gay. Suzanne explained that it wasn't a choice and that it could be scary at times because people would judge you and make life hard for you. But, if you want to live an authentic life, she said, you have to accept who you are and learn to embrace it.

During college I shared a house with my best friend, Monique (straight as an arrow), and a couple of other women. During my senior year, as curious as I'd ever been, I went with Suzanne to a gay bar in downtown Providence. Monique asked me where I was going and I told her the library. That night I met and kissed a girl who had short pink hair and rode a motorcycle. I must've told her that I played lacrosse for Brown, because she showed up at my game the next day. I was walking off the field with my teammates when I heard the woman with pink hair yelling my name as she waved in my direction. "Who's *that*?" asked one of my teammates. This woman looked the part of a proud lesbian. "I have *no* idea; that is *so* weird," I said, doing my best to sound confused instead of panicky. The woman continued to shout my name, but I completely ignored her. She must've had the wrong Siri.

When my dad found out that I was gay, he was devastated. His wife had caught wind that I was dating someone in our shared lacrosse circle, and after she told my dad, he called me in tears. "Say it isn't true, Siri! I'm begging you! Tell me it's a lie." His reaction destroyed me. I knew that my dad had grown up in an era when being gay was considered an aberration and a sin—gay people were cloaked in shame—and I was willing to give him time to digest the truth and work through it. Surely he would still accept me as his devoted daughter—a father's love is unconditional.

But even over time, he couldn't handle it. He was ashamed, embarrassed, and disappointed. I was a good daughter, a star athlete, an Ivy League graduate, and a person who had earned the respect and admiration of her peers and friends. None of that mattered. Not helping the situation was his deeply homophobic wife, whose controlling influence sealed the lid of the coffin for our relationship. He made a choice to not muddy the waters in his new life, and that meant distancing himself from me.

My mom, on the other hand, was immensely supportive of me. I think she'd already known. We'd always been incredibly close, and she's a perceptive and intuitive person. We were in Maui on vacation, and we were walking on the beach when I felt an overwhelming impulse to confess to her.

"Mom, I'm gay," I said plainly. "I don't have a girlfriend, and I haven't been in a relationship, and that is why I am so certain that this is true. I'm not being influenced by anyone. I have realized totally on my own that this is who I am. Please don't stop loving me."

M had tears in her eyes. They weren't sad tears—she went on to tell me that she was profoundly proud of me.

"I know it must've taken a lot of courage to get those words out," she said. "You must have struggled a lot in trying to understand your feelings, and all I want for you is to be happy—to be *you*."

The wave of relief was bigger than any Hawaiian surf behemoth.

M said she worried, though, that I would be treated unfairly or perhaps discriminated against when it came to jobs or other opportunities. I told her I wouldn't let that happen. I would get so good at whatever I did that people would have no choice but to accept me—just like in college, when I went up against my field hockey coach and asserted, "I will do everything in my power to make sure you can't keep me on the bench." I was intensely motivated to not let anything or anyone determine the limits of my success.

When I started getting more heavily into triathlon, I was introduced to other gay women who supported my journey. I met girlfriends through the sport, including Kristy, who also got carbon dioxide poisoning on that drive to age-group nationals back in Maryland. Lynn, Yoli, and Jenny Rose were hugely supportive. The encouragement and friendship of strong, positive, and kind gay women in my early triathlon pursuits laid the foundation of my future success.

But as a lifelong people pleaser, I struggled with falling short of being the person I thought people wanted me to be. Sometimes my inner discord created confusion and pain for people I really cared about. My friend Grant was one of those people. He was a great swimmer and swim coach in Boulder, and he would sometimes train with me during my visits there. After I retired and started coaching, he would help me with my athletes at their training sessions, acting like an assistant coach. He was a quality guy, someone I could talk to and lean on. I knew he really cared about me, and part of me felt like I owed it to him to consider him romantically. I kissed him at a Christmas party, and we started dating. Six months later, we were at dinner with a group of my close friends and family, and to my total surprise, he proposed in front of everyone. I was so shocked, and felt cornered in the situation with all of our friends excitedly looking on, that I said yes. I knew it was the wrong answer, but I didn't know how to pump the brakes. Once we were engaged, he moved in with me. I wish I'd had the nerve and self-confidence to not let things get so far out of control.

There were many signs that my heart wasn't in it. Loretta and Annie came to visit me, and I would make an elaborate dinner for them every night while Grant was still at work. He'd come through the door, and I'd toss a burger or bratwurst on the grill for him. He was happy enough, but Loretta and Annie would ask me how I could treat him so inconsiderately. I was just that checked out.

When Christmas came again, Grant left town to be with his family, and I went to M's house. It was Christmas Eve, and we were sitting in her living room when my mom said, "You must be missing

Grant and so sad to be apart on Christmas." I broke into tears. "It's terrible, but I'm happier when we're apart," I told her. I could not have asked for a better man or partner than Grant, which only made it more apparent that it was my issue, not his. I knew that night I had to break things off. I felt terrible that I'd hurt him in my hopeless effort to suppress a fundamental self-truth.

After I came out to my dad, I didn't see him for a few years. He and his wife were raising two young sons, and he was entirely focused on his new family. Still, right after I retired, I went to Connecticut to spend a weekend with him in an effort to repair some of the damage. When his wife took me up to the room I'd be staying in, it was dirty, and the walls were filled with photos of my stepbrothers. There wasn't a single photo of Lisa or me. I was heartbroken that he couldn't make the simple effort of cleaning the guest room—at least changing the dirty sheets—or hanging a single photo of us among the hundreds of framed pictures of his boys. I walked through every room in the house looking for a reminder that I existed and didn't find one.

His weekend plan was to watch the boys at their hockey games and shuttle them to practices and play dates. I'd never felt so alone, so unwanted. I left the next morning to go stay with Pat Brown and his boyfriend in New York City. My dad felt bad and came into the city a couple of days later to meet me. We sat in a quiet restaurant, and he told me that his wife didn't like him spending time with my sister or me. He was crying and seemed genuinely distraught. But when I asked him to put his foot down and tell her he wouldn't abandon his daughters, he said he couldn't do that. He needed to keep the peace in his marriage. I couldn't understand how he could turn his back on us and concluded that he felt we just weren't worth it.

Despite the rejection, I ultimately found peace within myself. When Brett e-mailed me in 2006 to ask about another Olympics bid, one of my reasons for saying no was that I'd finally found some serenity in my life—I didn't need to chase triathlon goals to find contentment. "I am finally living my truth, at least with myself, my family, and the people I care about the most in my life," I told him. "I am more confident in me as a human being and what I can offer to those relationships that are of great value to me. I don't have to hide myself; I am me and thus feel so free and fulfilled with my relationships for the first time in my life." I didn't need to seek my self-worth in sport any longer, and that came from accepting who I was as a person.

After my toxic Los Angeles relationship ended, I didn't want to be with anyone for a while. I felt like I'd been put through the emotional and financial wringer, and I needed to sort out my own life.

And then Rebekah Keat turned my life inside out in the best possible way.

I first met Bek, an Australian, in 1999 when we were both in Australia racing triathlon professionally. I was training in Cronulla, renting a room in Michellie Jones's house—I wanted to be the kind of champion Michellie was, and I studied her every move—and Bek came over to train for the day. She had been racing triathlon at the elite level since her junior years, and I had a lot of respect for her as an athlete. Bek was friendly and easy to talk to—her personality made her immediately likable. We continued to see each other occasionally at races—I was always excited to say hello and make a connection—but the friendship remained casual. After I retired from triathlon, I continued to take my athletes to Australia to train. One day, I was with my squad at the pool where Bek was training. We sat down and shared our longest conversation yet, during which she told me she was gay. She explained how hard it was, but she was in a relationship and had decided she needed to start living honestly. I was impressed with the strength she showed in overcoming her fear of being judged and opting instead to live true to herself. We became a bit closer through this conversation, and over the years, whenever I was in Australia, we would get together for dinner.

I witnessed Bek in two other relationships during that time. I had no romantic thoughts toward her at this point; I just liked knowing her and was always excited to spend time with her. In Kona in 2009, after Rinny won, I was ecstatic. I ran into Bek as I was heading back to the condo after the race, and she was in tears. She'd had one of her best races but had been disqualified (she crossed the center line of the road on her bike while coming into transition but wasn't notified of her disqualification until after completing the marathon), taking away her fifth place finish. She was with her twin sister, Simone, or Simmy, and I saw the pain in Bek's eyes and tears streaming down her face. It broke my heart. I didn't know her very well, but I remember being affected by her situation—I could almost feel her pain. I gave her a hug and told her how sorry I was.

Three years later, in 2012, Bek asked me to coach her. She'd been training with Brett and said she was tired of waking up nearly in tears not knowing what kind of pain was in store for the day, a feeling I knew all too well. He had her doing six Ironman races over the course of three or four months, and she was battling chronic injury. When she came to me, I was excited. I didn't know if it was because she was such an incredible athlete with so much promise or if there was something more. Maybe both. One thing was certain: I'd never violated the coach-athlete rule before and wasn't about to now.

I wanted to be the very best coach I could be for her. I wanted to impress Bek and make choosing me the best decision she'd ever made. Our first training camp together was in Noosa, Australia. When I arrived at the house where I'd be staying, a pro named Amanda Balding, who'd set up the housing arrangements, said, "I'm so sorry, I know you wanted to live alone. This is a huge house, and you will have the upstairs, but Rebekah Keat will be staying downstairs. I hope that's okay?" Normally I would have been annoyed, as I never shared living space with my athletes, but I was uncharacteristically fine with it.

Throughout that camp, we spent many evenings together cooking dinner and watching TV. We talked for hours, and I not only saw the Bek that I had always really liked—funny, interesting, smart, kind, and gregarious—but I also saw another side of her, a deep and sensitive soul. She was caring and in touch with the things that really mattered: family, friends, and finding joy in simple things. We made each other laugh, and, most importantly, we inspired one another.

We were falling in love, but it was under the wrong circumstances. I would never allow myself to be romantically involved with one of my athletes. Plus, Bek was in a relationship—she was unhappy but not technically available. Falling for Bek was unexpected, but it happened, and we knew that if we wanted to explore the possibilities, we had many obstacles to overcome. Neither of us had ever experienced the depth of feelings that our growing bond was bringing us, so we decided to tackle everything before us to make our dream of being together come true. Bek spent months dealing with the breakup of her own relationship—she and her ex, like me and mine, had to sort out ugly logistical and financial complications—and, like me, she lost much in the fallout. But that cost was trivial compared to the sense of freedom it allowed us to finally be together. I was full of trepidation, especially because I was breaking my own rule about not dating one of my athletes, but Bek reassured me at every turn, rebuilt my trust, and made me feel like she would do anything to fight for our relationship. No one had ever gone through such hardship—or been so patient and determined—to be with me, and her steadfast faith in our relationship over the course of the next year earned my confidence as well.

Bek is the love of my life. She gets me like no one ever has. She appreciates me for all that I am. Her love opened my eyes to what being happy really means—feeling truly safe with someone. It is the love that I dreamed about as a little girl—something that seemed like an impossible fairy tale. When you find a love like that, a love that gives meaning to everything in your life, you want people to know. You want to celebrate it every single day. All of my shame and insecurity about being gay were washed away. I had never felt my feet so solidly planted on the ground; I had never felt my heart so open and unafraid.

Bek didn't think she'd ever get married—we were both so gun-shy after failed relationships—but after two years of dating, she saw that possibility with me. She proposed in Waikiki on October 4, 2015. She'd written, "Will you marry me?" in rocks on the beach, but the tide came in and messed it up, so instead she hung my ring on the branch of a banyan tree. She put on a beautiful dress and asked me to come outside. She was trembling from nervousness, and halfway through her speech, I blurted out, "Yes! I will marry you!" I never even gave her a chance to ask the question.

Two months later, we were married at 4 in the afternoon in Estes Park, Colorado. It was just the minister and the two of us. We taped our wedding on an iPhone using a selfie stick and sent the video to our families and closest friends. It was 20 degrees outside, but I don't remember ever feeling cold. It was the best day of my life.

The following May, M hosted a perfect wedding reception for us. She put her heart and soul into it and was proud to have her extended family there to celebrate our union. Seeing her genuinely excited and happy for us made my heart sing. My dad came and gave a toast, which was something I would never have imagined could happen. Although we don't talk, I know Dad reads up on triathlon and my athletes, and, deep down, he does feel love and pride for me.

A few years ago, I tattooed the word "believe" on the inside of my left wrist and "gratitude" on the inside of my right one. These are the guiding words in my life, the themes of my chosen script. I strive to live every moment of each day with a heart full of gratitude for the countless moments of grace and tremendous blessings in my life, big and small, past and present. And I am an unabashed believer in the magic that can happen in the relentless, fearless, heart-guided pursuit of a dream held tight.

I believe that every person is a rare work of art, like a magnificent sculpture just waiting to emerge from an amorphous slab of rock. The process of chipping away to reveal the beauty and truth buried within is a lifelong undertaking. Sometimes progress is painfully slow and gets derailed by setbacks. Other times you're pleasantly surprised and forever changed by what you find.

I promise you this: If you are committed with all of your being to the pursuit of your dream—to the unearthing of your true self and potential—you will be blinded by the brilliant light that emerges when you are cracked open.

EPILOGUE

MY TRIATHLON DREAM was everything to me—it saved me from myself and gave me life. That is why when an athlete comes to me with a goal, I don't take it lightly. This person is entrusting me with his or her dream. Regardless of how ambitious the goal is or how high the stakes, when someone expresses their faith in me to help them, I am honored. The first order of business is determining what it will take to get from point A to point B. Sometimes it's just a matter of following a methodical plan, and other times it includes a significant sacrifice on both sides.

Once both of us commit to the goal, I invest 100 percent—from a time and energy perspective but also mentally. As soon as I say I'm in, that athlete is my responsibility. I want it as much as they want it, and I don't want to let anyone down, including myself. I ask the athlete to get better every day—to make incremental improvements by working hard and being focused—and I have the same expectation of myself. It's only fair.

When I first started coaching athletes, there was a perception that since I was Brett Sutton's protégée, I would hammer my athletes. But I didn't set out to blindly adhere to one style or approach. That's not to say I didn't adopt some of Brett's principles. More than anything, I want to give an athlete confidence that he or she already has the tools needed to achieve excellence. Sometimes it's necessary to have a guide, like Brett was for me, to show you how to find the tools and use them. But once athletes realize that everything they need already lies within, they feel accountable and empowered. Then it comes down to channeling all the focus, energy, and commitment toward that goal. If you do this, "success becomes inevitable," as Brett would say.

My coaching philosophy is rooted in the foundational belief that facing your fears head-on will result in performance breakthroughs. Pushing your body to new physical extremes can be seriously uncomfortable. But the better an athlete becomes at facing that fear—embracing it, even—the sooner he or she will realize that it's possible to push beyond anticipated limits. Countless times, Brett delivered the same message: You can always go farther, you can always get faster, stronger, and fitter—it is only the mind that turns on the red light. There will be tough workouts when an athlete has to really dig deep, believe, and not give up when the pain seems too much. The athlete can respond in one of two ways: Yield to the pain and self-doubt or decide that fear will not determine his or her potential. It's hard (and usually uncomfortable) work breaking through old barriers and self-defeating thought patterns to see meaningful progress, and fear is an absolutely natural response, but you can't let it become a limiter. Brett took the time to figure me out as a person and pinpoint exactly what I needed to have that breakthrough. Oftentimes what gets in the way of the best performance has nothing to do with the physical preparation.

Taking mind, body, and spirit into account is what gets results. I don't train just the physical body—I have to take the person's emotional life into account and figure out how to work around any mental blocks. I strive to get inside my athletes' heads to help them perform to their true potential. A keen emotional intelligence (something that is often underestimated) paired with a deep understanding of the complex physiological mechanisms and adaptations at play makes for a powerfully effective coach. I see every athlete as a multilayered human being and take a holistic approach to coaching. Like Yoli, I encourage my athletes to focus on being good people, because when you nurture a strong character, work ethic, sense of respect, and gratitude, the results will follow.

I've worked with a number of athletes who have trained under both Brett and me, and one difference that always emerges is my relentless positivity. I'm all about positive reinforcement and trying to glean joy, gratitude, and purpose from every moment, even the tough ones. It's not about putting on a happy face to project a certain image, and it's certainly not simply serving as a cheerleader for my athletes—that characterization has always irked me. I truly believe that attitude is a choice and energy is infectious. I *choose* to focus on the positive and nurture an uplifting environment. I've always been ultracommitted to creating a harmonious squad dynamic. A healthy and happy team is a sacred thing, and I protect it like a mama bear safeguarding her cubs.

Being positive and being tough are not mutually exclusive qualities in a coach. I firmly believe you can earn the respect of your athletes without acting in a way that compromises your values. You can deliver a tough message with both honesty and sensitivity. When Brett told me I had to lose weight, he did it in a way that had lasting effects on my body image. The truth is, before that humiliating interaction on the pool deck when I first arrived at camp, I had never worried about what I looked like in a bathing suit. To this day, I won't be caught dead in a swimsuit, even at the beach in the middle of summer. I know I'm in shape because I make fitness a priority in my life, but I still hear that voice in my head telling me my ass looks like "rabbits in a sack." I accept that his unsparing critiques were intended to get my attention and that ultimately he was trying to help me—and he did. But as a coach, I know there is a better way.

I think some people discount my toughness and effectiveness because of my "bubbly" exterior or "rose-colored glasses." Being underestimated is actually a great motivator for me—always has been, always will be. Nothing fires me up more than being underrated. I try to encourage my athletes to approach any doubters in the same way—use that doubt to stoke your ambition. I derive a lot of satisfaction from the deep bonds I have with my athletes. I'm not talking about a best-friend relationship where you know the ins and outs of each other's personal lives. I have a precise agenda: understanding what makes my athlete tick. To do that, I need to build mutual trust and respect with an athlete in a way that allows me to coax out his or her true potential. I celebrate my athletes' victories—large and small—as if they are my own, because they *are* also mine.

I haven't always been transparent about the specifics of my coaching methodology—which makes sense in a competitive landscape—and because I don't talk a lot about training with data, there's a tendency to think I'm not a "numbers person." While I do believe there is value in training with heart rate monitors and power meters, athletes often fall into the trap of depending too heavily on metrics. It's easy to fixate on number readings, which can put a ceiling on effort. An athlete will think, *Great, I'm right where I need to be*, and settle into the effort. But often when you are training blind—guided instead by perceived effort—you can draw more out of yourself. If you went out to do a bike workout that included 30 minutes at functional threshold power/threshold effort, you would probably use your power meter to make sure you were riding that half hour right at your threshold pace. But what would happen if you didn't use your power meter and rode as hard as you could sustain for that 30-minute window? Would your numbers be higher than when you rode guided by your power ceiling? Free your mind of the data focus, and you will be blown away by your ability to exceed expectations. People are often much more powerful than they think they are.

The mental aspect allows people to break barriers, win races, and achieve their true potential. I constantly challenge my athletes with workouts that take them to the upper edge of their ability. Like Brett's, my philosophy is that your biggest competitor is yourself. I will never ask the impossible. But I will come close. Those who answer with courage and self-belief instead of fear and doubt are the ones who realize their dreams.

My instincts have served me well in life, and that's especially true when deciding to take on a pro athlete. Is this person 100 percent invested in his or her dream? Is this person willing to do the work, year after year if necessary, with a positive and hopeful attitude toward the team? Will this person make every necessary sacrifice? I need to have complete confidence that the answer to those questions is a definitive yes. And if it is, then I believe with all my being that the dream is achievable. I am living proof that it is.

Sometimes athletes hit a plateau and begin to question whether it's the end of the road. Having stood at that crossroads myself, wondering which direction to take, I like to be sure I've explored every option. I don't think it's ever too late to rethink or recalibrate your approach to achieving your dream. I've had a number of top pro triathletes come to me as a last resort before walking away from the sport. Two-time Olympian Sam Warriner was about to give up, but after getting excited and inspired again, she raced to an ITU World Cup Series champion title in 2008. British star Leanda "Bird" Cave (who won the 2002 ITU world championship in Cancún, my last pro race) was beginning to lose interest when she came to me in 2010. Even Brett said, "Bird's done." She wanted to be better than ever and get her passion back and was willing to do anything it took to make it happen. We went all in and achieved a historic milestone together. It was the same story for Dutch long-course pro Yvonne van Vlerken—

she was ready to retire, and with my help, she completely turned things around. I won't give up on anyone; as long as an athlete's full devotion and drive toward a goal remain, I am equally relentless.

But sometimes, for whatever reason, an athlete will decide to give up on the coach and move on. (Brett did warn me.) These decisions used to devastate me—each one felt like a breakup. But then I realized I'd done my job—I'd given that person my heart and soul—and should be satisfied by what we'd been able to accomplish. Most of the time, we had achieved whatever they had come to me for, and it was just time for a different experience.

Consider someone like Sarah True, whom I coached for four years. She came to me when she was still new to the sport; she lacked self-belief but had great potential and was willing to work hard. I was her Yoli. We made some great strides, but there was one thing holding her back. If something started to go wrong in a race, she would give up. I would say, "You can't give up in that moment—it's not over; you just need to compose yourself." I couldn't get that message through to her, but her current coach somehow did. I watched Sarah run in the 2012 Olympics; when she got dropped, I thought, *If she reacts the way I think she will, her race is over*. But she kept her head in the race and clawed her way back to put herself in medal contention. She finished just off the podium in fourth, but I cried happy tears because she'd hurdled her biggest limiter. I was tremendously proud of her.

One of my top Ironman racers left because her old coach had gotten in her head. She said, "I'm training better than ever and seeing numbers that I've never seen before, but I can't move beyond the fact that [my former coach] said I'd never win without him." I told her she had two choices: Take the time to overcome this mental block and lack of self-belief and realize she could do it without him, or go back. She said she didn't have the inner strength for the first option, and the clock on her pro career was ticking, so she went back to him. Within two weeks, she was winning again. That was hard, but after her win, she wrote to me and said I was part of that victory. That's the type of athlete I'm grateful for: one who understands how much I'm investing in him or her. My longtime athlete Yvonne van Vlerken is perhaps the best example of gratitude in action—it makes me want to work even harder for her.

As tough as it is when a team member leaves, there have been times when it has been a blessing in disguise. I had one athlete who believed she raced better when she was pissed and miserable. What kind of atmosphere do you think that mentality created for her teammates? A gloomy or selfish presence in the group can compromise everyone's success. When that negative person is gone, all of a sudden the morale and energy in the room feel lighter. There is a renewed optimism that everyone can harness.

When I know that every person wants to be there, is entirely committed, and appreciates the team, there's nothing holding me back from giving every ounce of my soul.

It's not uncommon for champions to emerge from a place of brokenness. I believe that my own experiences, however painful, ultimately shaped me. Looking back on my life, I wouldn't change a thing. Every tough time I have ever worked through has only made me stronger and more resolute. The people who have hurt me have actually helped me. Each time you suffer—in sport or life—you come back stronger, with a thicker skin and greater wisdom. Enduring hardship can be brutal, but when you emerge from it, there is something positive to be gleaned from every situation. If you sincerely believe that, you can brave any difficulty.

My mom is the best living example of this tenet. I now know how hard those years with Frank were for my mom (both during and after the marriage) and have great respect for her strength, resilience, and resolve to make a better life for herself and her daughters. She has always held her head high, unwilling to be a victim of circumstance, even in the face of the most formidable challenge. Her precedent has always inspired me to attempt to do the same.

My destiny began to change when I made the decision that I didn't want to feel bad anymore, when I began to believe that I deserved to be happy. My older sister, Lisa, experienced the same challenges growing up, but she has been on a very different journey. It's gutting to see someone you love and revere struggle with addiction and inner turmoil. My deepest hope is that she can find the resolve and clarity to choose a path of love, not fear, and peace instead of unrest.

I've been blessed to have people believe in me long before I saw any potential in myself. I remember thinking, *If they believe in me for some reason, maybe I need to start believing, too.* And I've always felt the presence of God and an acute awareness of His grace in my life. My faith has brought me comfort my entire life, as I've carried a belief that God loves us all, no matter what. He gives me strength and brings me hope—always. I yearn to show my gratitude for the life I live and the people with whom I share it, and I thank God for the amazing blessings of my inner strength, my determination, and the great opportunities I have been lucky enough to have in my life. I thank God for my arms, my legs, my beating heart, and the continual stream of dreams and visions, goals and passions. I pray that I can show gratitude for my amazing blessings by being the very best person that I can be every single day of my life—by bringing joy, love, and support to those around me and inspiring others to be the very best that they can be.

ACKNOWLEDGMENTS

First and foremost, I want to thank my amazing mom, who has been there since day one protecting, supporting, guiding, calming, and loving me. I would not have been able to achieve the things I did without your support and inspiration, M. Sharing my life and travels with you is something that I will cherish forever. You are my best friend and greatest mentor, and I love you with all of my soul.

I have my father to thank for lighting my athletic fire. From a very young age, I was always doing something active with him—baseball, football, pond hockey, lacrosse, ice skating, and tennis. His passion for sports deeply influenced me, and he helped me become the athlete I eventually grew into. He encouraged me to believe that I could be as good as I wanted to be, as long as I was willing to work for it. Thank you, Dad, for your limitless support in the first 21 years of my life. Although we have been through hard times, I pray that someday we can mend our relationship. I will always love you with all my heart.

My sister, Lisa, and I have been through a lot together. Lisa, I looked up to you so much as a child and only ever wanted to be half as good as you in all the sports we loved. You have a brilliant mind, a beautiful heart, and a loving soul. I pray that you can realize this one day and give yourself the life I know you are capable of creating.

Anyone who knows me understands my love for my animals—those that have passed and those that are still with me. They have always been my security blanket and loved me unconditionally when I felt unlovable. Animals have been great teachers for me, showing me how to find great joy in the smallest things, to love and forgive, and to appreciate. I have drawn strength and inspiration from Charlie, Fifi, Susie, Dribble, Panda, Lulu, Whoopi, Gertie, Billy, Sophie, Athena, and Gracie—and, still with me, Calvin, Byron, Sparky, Vinnie, and Savannah, as well as M's endless generations of pugs.

Thank you to Julia Beeson Polloreno for all of the heart and soul you put into the creation of my book. From the beginning, I felt an amazing connection with you, my "soul sister." You get me and all my complexities. You made me feel safe, which in turn inspired me to share all of me without hesitation. Thank you for your hard work, your understanding, your wisdom, and your heart. You truly are a champion of the human spirit, and I couldn't have done this without you!

Thank you to the VeloPress crew for believing my story was worthy of sharing and that it could serve as a beacon of hope and inspiration for others. I am grateful to Renee Jardine, whose gentle and thoughtful guidance and all-around editorial smarts were instrumental.

I have been fortunate to have many mentors, people who have helped fuel my passion and bolster my self-belief. Oh, how I miss you, Coach Renee Spellman. You saved me and gave me direction when I needed it most. I cannot thank you enough for encouraging me to believe, even at such a young age, that one day I could not only be great at something but learn to authentically love and accept myself. There are countless others I've had the good fortune to learn from, either by example or direct influence. They include Marvin Bush, Mark Allen, Scott Tinley, Paula Newby-Fraser, Karen Smyers, Wendy Ingraham, Michellie Jones, and Tony Robbins.

To all the coaches who helped mold me into the athlete I became and the coach I am now, thank you. Whether the lessons were easily accepted and happily applied or given in a tough-love way that got through to me, each lesson helped make me who I am today. Thank you for caring enough to be hard on me and for challenging me to face my fears, dig deeper, and become better every single day. I am forever indebted to Yoli Casas, Jack Ralston, Lynn Oski, and Jane Scott as well as Carolan Norris, Wendy Anderson, Digit Murphy, Chris Sailer, Beth Bozman, Jenny Rose, and Jackie Keeley. Thank you, Brett Sutton, for accessing the deepest recesses of my psyche and finding a way to set me free from the fears that had a stranglehold on my life.

Karen Burks, thank you for helping me manage the business side of my job. You have been not just my athlete but an incredible friend and adviser over the past 10 years. Your wisdom and strength are awe-inspiring.

Thank you to my athletes, past and present. We have shared amazing times and achieved incredible things. I grew so much from my time with each and every one of you. There are a handful of athletes in particular whom I'd like to recognize for giving me so much joy and gratification as a coach: Mirinda Carfrae, Yvonne van Vlerken, Rebekah Keat, Leanda Cave, Cliff Adlerz, Ellie Salthouse, Susan Williams, Sarah (Groff) True, Hillary Biscay, Gunzy Groves, Mary Beth Ellis, Rafael Gonçalves, Chris Foster, Luke McKenzie, Jill Savege, Sam Warriner, and Marcela Miramontes.

To the friends who have stood by my side, inspired me, and accepted me, I am deeply grateful. Annie Emmerson, Patrick Brown, Simone Keat, Monique Kapitulik, Kerry Bozza, Yoli Casas, Erin Carson, and Melissa Lindamood—you are friends for a lifetime.

My very best friend in the world, Loretta Harrop, gave me the opportunity to train with her and Brett, and I will be forever thankful. Not only did you help me achieve my greatest dreams in the sport but you became my most devoted friend, someone I looked up to and respected as a person and an athlete. You made me a better person. I love you, my friend, and you are truly one of the strongest women I have known!

I am so thankful to my beautiful wife, Rebekah Keat. I never thought I would find a love that filled my heart and made me feel special, appreciated, and adored. You have held my heart tenderly, calmed my fears, and shown me in infinite ways how much you love me. Thank you for making me laugh every single day, for inspiring me to be the very best person that I can be. Your kind and loving heart and giving soul make me proud. I have never met anyone else with your passion, generosity, and zest for life. I love you with all of my being.

Thank you to my second family, Ruth and Simone Keat. You have welcomed me into your family and supported the love I share with your daughter—it means everything to me.

RACE RESULTS

SIRI LINDLEY'S CAREER HIGHLIGHTS

1996

1ST // Pucón International Triathlon, CHL, 2:40:24
7TH // St. Anthony's Triathlon, St. Petersburg, FL, 2:06:29
16TH // ITU Triathlon World Cup, Hamilton, BMU, 1:56:58
29TH // **ITU Triathlon World Championship**, Cleveland, OH, 1:58:45
14TH // ITU Triathlon World Cup, Noosa, AUS, 2:05:08

1997

12TH // ITU Triathlon World Cup, Cancún, MEX, 2:04:21
22ND // **ITU Triathlon World Championship**, Perth, AUS, 2:04:10

1998

7TH // PATCO Triathlon North American Championships, Los Cabos, MEX, 2:15:01
15TH // **ITU Triathlon World Championship**, Lausanne, CHE, 2:12:35
6TH // ITU Triathlon World Cup, Cancún, MEX, 2:05:15
1ST // USA Triathlon National Championship, Oceanside, CA, 2:05:30

7TH // ITU Triathlon World Cup, Auckland, NZL, 2:01:43
13TH // ITU Triathlon World Cup, Noosa, AUS, 2:04:13

1999

10TH // ITU Triathlon World Cup, Ishigaki, JPN, 2:02:29
4TH // ITU Triathlon World Cup, Gamagori, JPN, 1:55:26
4TH // ITU Triathlon World Cup, Sydney, AUS, 2:04:24
5TH // ITU Triathlon World Cup, Kapelle-op-den-Bos, BEL, 1:57:36
5TH // ITU Triathlon World Cup, Monte Carlo, MCO, 2:03:02
8TH // ITU Triathlon World Cup, Tiszaújváros, HUN, 1:59:04
4TH // ITU Triathlon World Cup, Noosa, AUS, 1:56:40
3RD // ITU World Cup Triathlon series

2000

10TH // **ITU Triathlon World Championship**, Perth, AUS, 1:56:01
3RD // USA Triathlon Olympic Trials, Dallas, TX, 2:07:35
6TH // ITU Triathlon World Cup, Toronto, CAN, 1:58:48
2ND // ITU Triathlon World Cup, Tiszaújváros, HUN, 1:55:16
1ST // ITU Triathlon World Cup, Lausanne, CHE, 2:05:22
3RD // Mrs. T's Chicago Triathlon, IL, 2:00:14
2ND // ITU Duathlon World Championship, Calais, FRA, 2:02:03
1ST // ITU Triathlon World Cup, Cancún, MEX, 1:57:52

2001

6TH // ITU Triathlon World Cup, Gamagori, JPN, 1:58:26
3RD // ITU Triathlon World Cup, Ishigaki, JPN, 1:58:15
1ST // ITU Triathlon World Cup, Rennes, FRA, 1:59:32
1ST // ITU Triathlon World Cup, Toronto, CAN, 2:00:04
1ST // ITU Aquathlon World Championship, Edmonton, CAN, 25:09
1ST // **ITU Triathlon World Championship**, Edmonton, CAN, 1:58:50
1ST // ITU Triathlon World Cup, Corner Brook, CAN, 2:03:16
1ST // ITU Triathlon World Cup, Tiszaújváros, HUN, 1:56:47
1ST // ITU Triathlon World Cup, Lausanne, CHE, 2:07:08
4TH // Goodwill Games Triathlon, Brisbane, AUS, 2:02:42
1ST // ITU World Cup Triathlon series

2002

1ST // OTU Triathlon Oceania Cup, Devonport, AUS, 2:02:21
3RD // ITU Triathlon World Cup, Geelong, AUS, 2:03:05
7TH // ITU Triathlon World Cup, Ishigaki, JPN, 2:02:17
1ST // ITU Triathlon World Cup, Edmonton, CAN, 2:01:33
1ST // ITU Triathlon World Cup, Corner Brook, CAN, 2:05:43
1ST // ITU Triathlon World Cup, Tiszaújváros, HUN,1:57:04
1ST // ETU Triathlon European Cup, Geneva, CHE, 2:18:07
1ST // ITU Triathlon World Cup, Lausanne, CHE, 2:02:42
2ND // ITU Triathlon World Cup, Hamburg, DEU, 1:57:56
13TH // **ITU Triathlon World Championship**, Cancún, MEX, 2:04:10
1ST // ITU World Cup Triathlon series

COACHING HIGHLIGHTS

2003

SAVEGE, 1ST // ITU Triathlon World Cup, Corner Brook, CAN, 2:05:26
SAVEGE, 1ST // Pan American Games, Santo Domingo, DOM, 1:59:30

2004

HARROP, SILVER // Olympic Games—triathlon, Athens, GRC, 2:04:50
WILLIAMS, BRONZE // Olympic Games—triathlon, Athens, GRC, 2:05:08
BENNIGSON, 1ST // US Elite National Triathlon Champion
ROWE, 1ST // US Pro Duathlon National Champion

2006

CARFRAE, 4TH // ITU Triathlon World Cup, Ishigaki, JPN, 1:58:58
CARFRAE, 1ST // Ironman 70.3 St. Croix, VIR, 4:30:13
CARFRAE, 1ST // Ironman 70.3 Baja, Ensenada, MEX, 4:31:13
GROVES, 4TH // **ITU Triathlon World Championship**, Lausanne, CHE, 2:05:24
CARFRAE, 3RD // **Ironman 70.3 World Championship**, Clearwater, FL, 4:16:44

2007

CARFRAE, 5TH // City of Perth Triathlon, AUS, 1:04:51
CARFRAE, 4TH // St. Anthony's Triathlon, St. Petersburg, FL, 2:00:18
CARFRAE, 2ND // Wildflower, Lake San Antonio, CA, 4:38:14

TRUE, 1ST // ITU Aquathlon World Championship, Ixtapa, MEX, 32:52
CARFRAE, 2ND // Ironman 70.3 Eagleman, Cambridge, MD, 4:13:19
CARFRAE, 2ND // Ironman 70.3 Buffalo Springs Lake, TX, 4:20:06
GROVES, 3RD // Pan American Games, Rio de Janeiro, BRA, 1:59:50
CARFRAE, 7TH // Minneapolis Life Time Fitness Triathlon, MN, 2:05:20
CARFRAE, 1ST // Spirit of Racine Half-Ironman, WI, 4:16:43
CARFRAE, 5TH // Chicago Triathlon, IL, 2:04:07
CARFRAE, 2ND // Ironman 70.3 Singapore, SGP, 4:17:17
CARFRAE, 3RD // Los Angeles Triathlon, CA, 2:07:17
CARFRAE, 3RD // US Open Triathlon, Dallas, TX, 1:59:11
CARFRAE, 1ST // **Ironman 70.3 World Championship**, Clearwater, FL, 4:07:25
CARFRAE, 1ST // St. Croix Triathlon, VIR, 2:17:12
CARFRAE, 2ND // Laguna Phuket Triathlon, THA, 2:44:28

2008

CARFRAE, 1ST // Ironman 70.3 Geelong, AUS, 4:24:27
CARFRAE, 2ND // Ironman 70.3 Oceanside, CA, 4:25:51
CARFRAE, 1ST // Aflac Iron Girl Lake Las Vegas, NV, 1:56:22
TRUE, 3RD // USA Triathlon Olympic Trials, Tuscaloosa, AL, 2:02:59
CARFRAE, 3RD // St. Anthony's Triathlon, St. Petersburg, FL, 2:01:52
CARFRAE, 1ST // Ironman 70.3 St. Croix, VIR, 4:33:39
CARFRAE, 3RD // Escape from Alcatraz Triathlon, San Francisco, CA, 2:16:47
GROVES, 14TH // BG Triathlon World Championship, Hamburg, DEU, 1:56:01
CARFRAE, 1ST // Battle at Midway Triathlon, UT, 2:04:56
CARFRAE, 1ST // Ironman 70.3 Buffalo Springs Lake, TX, 4:23:28
CARFRAE, 1ST // Newfoundland Ironman 70.3, Corner Brook, CAN, 4:27:23
CARFRAE, 5TH // Los Angeles Triathlon, CA, 2:06:50
TRUE, 2ND // World Cup Triathlon, Huatulco, MEX, 2:14:45
CARFRAE, 1ST // St. Croix Triathlon, VIR, 2:20:27
CARFRAE, 2ND // Laguna Phuket Triathlon, THA, 2:50:02
WARRINER, 1ST // ITU World Cup Triathlon series
TRUE, 4TH // ITU World Cup Triathlon series

2009

FOSTER, 1ST // ITU Triathlon Pan American Cup, Lima, PER, 1:58:15
CARFRAE, 1ST // Ironman 70.3 Oceanside, CA, 4:25:02
CARFRAE, 2ND // Ironman 70.3 St. Croix, VIR, 4:35:21

CARFRAE, 1ST // Rev3 Half Quassy, Middlebury, CT, 4:27:26

CARFRAE, 1ST // Ironman 70.3 Eagleman, Cambridge, MD, 4:13:27

CARFRAE, 1ST // Aflac Iron Girl Atlanta, GA, 1:13:55

CARFRAE, 1ST // Ironman 70.3 Calgary, CAN, 4:11:05

CARFRAE, 1ST // Ironman 70.3 Muskoka, CAN, 4:24:48

CARFRAE, 2ND // **Ironman World Championship**, Kona, HI, 9:13:59

2010

FOSTER, 2ND // ITU Triathlon Pan American Cup, La Paz, BRA, 1:55:58

CARFRAE, 1ST // Ironman 70.3 Oceanside, CA, 4:20:29

CARFRAE, 2ND // St. Anthony's Triathlon, St. Petersburg, FL, 2:00:20

CARFRAE, 1ST // Rev3 Half Quassy, Middlebury, CT, 4:23:38

CARFRAE, 3RD // TriGrandPrix Basque Country, Zarautz, ESP, 4:22:33

CARFRAE, 1ST // Ironman 70.3 Vineman, Windsor, CA, 4:15:51

CARFRAE, 1ST // Ironman 70.3 Calgary, CAN, 4:21:32

CARFRAE, 1ST // Ironman 70.3 Muskoka, CAN, 4:28:36

CARFRAE, 1ST // **Ironman World Championship**, Kona, HI, 8:58:36

2011

CARFRAE, 2ND // Ironman New Zealand, Taupo, NZL, 9:31:33

CARFRAE, 1ST // Ironman 70.3 Oceanside, CA, 4:26:18

CAVE, 1ST // Wildflower, Lake San Antonio, CA, 4:27:58

CARFRAE, 3RD // Ironman 70.3 St. Croix, VIR, 4:36:01

CARFRAE, 2ND // Rev3 Half Quassy, Middlebury, CT, 4:26:24

CARFRAE, 1ST // Ironman 70.3 Eagleman, Cambridge, MD, 4:15:31

CARFRAE, 3RD // Ironman 70.3 Vineman, Windsor, CA, 4:17:49

CARFRAE, 2ND // Hy-Vee 5150 US Championship, Des Moines, IA, 1:59:20

CARFRAE, 2ND // **Ironman World Championship**, Kona, HI, 8:57:57

CAVE, 3RD // **Ironman World Championship**, Kona, HI, 9:03:29

MCKENZIE, 9TH // **Ironman World Championship**, Kona, HI, 8:29:42

CAVE, 1ST // Ironman 70.3 Miami, FL, 4:13:35

CAVE, 2ND // ITU Triathlon World Championship, Henderson, NV, 1:59:20

CAVE, 1ST // Ironman Arizona, Tempe, AZ, 8:49:00

2012

KEAT, 6TH // Ironman Melbourne, AUS, 9:13:43

CARFRAE, 3RD // Ironman Melbourne (Asia-Pacific Championship), AUS, 9:04:00

VAN VLERKEN, 2ND // Ironman 70.3 Texas (US Championship), Galveston, TX, 4:18:47

CARFRAE, 3RD // Ironman 70.3 New Orleans, LA, 3:47:28

MCKENZIE, 4TH // Ironman 70.3 Busselton, AUS, 4:00:51

VAN VLERKEN, 1ST // Curaçao International Triathlon, Nieuwpoort, CUW, 2:09:49

CARFRAE, 1ST // Rev3 Half Quassy, Middlebury, CT, 4:27:02

CAVE, 1ST // Escape from Alcatraz Triathlon, San Francisco, CA, 2:18:17

MCKENZIE, 2ND // Ironman 70.3 Cairns, AUS, 4:08:01

FOSTER, 2ND // 5150 New Orleans, LA, 1:58:27

KEAT, 6TH // Ironman 70.3 Vineman, Windsor, CA, 4:20:23

KEAT, 2ND // Ironman New York (US National Championship), NY, 9:13:24

VAN VLERKEN, 1ST // Trans Vorarlberg Triathlon, AUT, 5:04:17

CAVE, 1ST // **Ironman 70.3 World Championship**, Las Vegas, NV, 4:28:05

FOSTER, 1ST // Nautical Malibu Triathlon, CA, 1:49:52

VAN VLERKEN, 3RD // Ironman 70.3 Cozumel, MEX, 4:22:10

FOSTER, 1ST // 5150 Galveston, TX, 1:49:39

CAVE, 1ST // **Ironman World Championship**, Kona, HI, 9:15:54

CAVE, 1ST // Ironman 70.3 Miami, FL, 4:07:27

VAN VLERKEN, 2ND // Ironman 70.3 Austin, TX, 4:24:03

VAN VLERKEN, 1ST // Ironman Florida, Panama City, FL, 8:51:35

KEAT, 1ST // Ironman 70.3 Shepparton, AUS, 4:16:17

KEAT, 2ND // Ironman Western Australia, Busselton, AUS, 9:14:39

2013

VAN VLERKEN, 2ND // Abu Dhabi International Triathlon, ARE, 7:31:27

VAN VLERKEN, 2ND // Ironman Melbourne, AUS, 8:26:40

VAN VLERKEN, 1ST // Leipzig Half-Marathon, DEU, 1:17:20

FOSTER, 2ND // Rev3 Knoxville, TN, 1:51:16

VAN VLERKEN, 2ND // Ironman 70.3 Mallorca, ESP, 4:27:17

STEVENS, 1ST // Ironman Brazil, Florianopolis, BRA, 9:05:53

MCKENZIE, 1ST // Ironman Cairns, AUS, 8:17:43

VAN VLERKEN, 1ST // Challenge Kraichgau, DEU, 4:26:35

VAN VLERKEN, 1ST // Half Triathlon Stein, NLD, 4:38:28

VAN VLERKEN, 2ND // Challenge Roth, DEU, 8:46:22

CAVE, 1ST // Ironman 70.3 Boulder, CO, 4:17:26

KEAT, 2ND // Ironman Mont-Tremblant (North American Championship), CAN, 9:16:55

VAN VLERKEN, 1ST // Challenge Walchsee, AUT, 4:19:13
CARFRAE, 1ST // **Ironman World Championship**, Kona, HI, 8:52:14
MCKENZIE, 2ND // **Ironman World Championship**, Kona, HI, 8:15:19
VAN VLERKEN, 4TH // **Ironman World Championship**, Kona, HI, 9:04:34
KEAT, 1ST // Ironman 70.3 Austin, TX, 4:15:59
VAN VLERKEN, 1ST // Ironman Florida, Panama City, FL, 8:43:07
KEAT, 1ST // Ironman 70.3 Shepparton, AUS, 4:13:03
KEAT, 1ST // Ironman 70.3 Canberra, AUS, 4:25:57

2014

SWALLOW, 1ST // Ironman 70.3 South Africa, East London, ZAF, 4:37:01
SWALLOW, 4TH // Abu Dhabi International Triathlon, ARE, 7:45:35
KEAT, 4TH // Ironman Melbourne (Asia-Pacific Championship), AUS, 9:11:06
SWALLOW, 3RD // Ironman African Championship, Port Elizabeth, ZAF, 9:33:59
KEAT, 6TH // Ironman 70.3 St. George (North American Championship), UT, 4:25:22
SWALLOW, 2ND // Ironman 70.3 St. George (North American Championship), UT, 4:12:29
SWALLOW, 1ST // Ironman 70.3 Boulder, CO, 4:07:37
KEAT, 4TH // Ironman Boulder 70.3, CO, 4:13:23
CARFRAE, 1ST // Challenge Roth, DEU, 8:38:53
VAN VLERKEN, 1ST // Challenge Walchsee, AUT, 4:25:53
SWALLOW, 2ND // **Ironman 70.3 World Championship**, Mont-Tremblant, CAN, 4:11:43
VAN VLERKEN, 1ST // Ironman 70.3 Rügen, DEU, 4:20:20
CARFRAE, 1ST // **Ironman World Championship**, Kona, HI, 9:00:55
SWALLOW, 4TH // **Ironman World Championship**, Kona, HI, 9:10:19
VAN VLERKEN, 1ST // Ironman Florida, Panama City, FL, 8:01:47
KEAT, 6TH // Ironman 70.3 Mandurah (Australian Championship), AUS, 4:10:59

2015

SWALLOW, 1ST // Ironman 70.3 South Africa, East London, ZAF, 4:30:54
KEAT, 2ND // Ironman 70.3 Geelong (Australian Championship), AUS, 4:20:02
VAN VLERKEN, 2ND // Ironman Melbourne, AUS, 8:58:58
CARFRAE, 7TH // Ironman Melbourne, AUS, 9:08:39
SWALLOW, 1ST // Ironman African Championship, Port Elizabeth, ZAF, 9:26:56
VAN VLERKEN, 3RD // Ironman 70.3 Mallorca, ESP, 4:29:03

SWALLOW, 3RD // Ironman 70.3 St. George (North American Championship), UT, 4:21:32

CARFRAE, 3RD // Escape from Alcatraz Triathlon, San Francisco, CA, 2:15:32

VAN VLERKEN, 1ST // Challenge Roth, DEU, 8:50:53

CARFRAE, 3RD // Ironman 70.3 Vineman, Windsor, CA, 4:18:33

VAN VLERKEN, 1ST // Ironman Maastricht-Limburg, NLD, 9:39:24

CARFRAE, 2ND // Des Moines International Triathlon, IA, 2:02:47

VAN VLERKEN, 2ND // Ironman 70.3 Rügen, DEU, 4:27:59

VAN VLERKEN, 1ST // Ironman Barcelona, ESP, 8:46:44

VAN VLERKEN, 2ND // Ironman 70.3 Mandurah, AUS, 4:10:14

KEAT, 1ST // Challenge Shepparton, AUS, 4:13:47

VAN VLERKEN, 2ND // Challenge Shepparton, AUS, 4:16:11

VAN VLERKEN, 3RD // Ironman Western Australia, Busselton, AUS, 9:12:07

VAN VLERKEN, 2ND // Ironman 70.3 Ballarat, AUS, 4:15:15

2016

SALTHOUSE, 1ST // Challenge Melbourne, AUS, 4:11:03

VAN VLERKEN, 1ST // Challenge Wanaka, Lake Wanaka, NZL, 9:26:50

CARFRAE, 3RD // Ironman 70.3 Monterrey, MEX, 4:15:11

VAN VLERKEN, 1ST // Vlietloop Half Marathon, NLD, 1:17:01

VAN VLERKEN, 1ST // Challenge Rimini, ITA, 4:40:54

CARFRAE, 3RD // Ironman 70.3 Chattanoooga, TN, 4:19:32

SALTHOUSE, 1ST // Ironman 70.3 Boulder, CO, 4:11:43

VAN VLERKEN, 1ST // Triathlon Ingolstadt, DEU, 3:48:35

CARFRAE, 1ST // Ironman Austria, Klagenfurt, AUT, 8:41:17

VAN VLERKEN, 3RD // Challenge Roth, DEU, 8:49:35

CARFRAE, 1ST // Ironman 70.3 Timberman, Gilford, NH, 4:22:22